From the Garden to the Glory

A Christian journey through the Bible

TIMOTHY CROSS

DayOne

Flying over the Alps was one of the most incredible experiences in my life. The snow-covered peaks created great awe as I looked out of the plane window. From the Garden to the Glory is a book that will enable you to see the remarkable mountain peaks of the Bible. Each mountain peak makes Jesus Christ more real and alive in our lives. You will not be disappointed in joining Timothy Cross as he takes you from the account of Adam and Eve to the glory of Jesus in Revelation

Pastor Mark Booth
Detroit, Michigan
USA

First published in Great Britain in 2021 by
Day One, Ryelands Road, Leominster, HR6 8NZ
Email: sales@dayone.co.uk
Website: www.dayone.co.uk

British Library Cataloguing in Publication Data available

ISBN: 978-1-84625-708-7

Cover design by Kathryn Chedgzoy

Printed by 4edge

Dedication

With thanks to Almighty God for the
life, love and labours of my mother,
Margaret Edna Cross, who went to be
with Christ on 13th September 2021.

'Many women have done excellently, but
you surpass them all' (Proverbs 31:29).

Contents

There is no book like the Bible. Christians revere the Bible because it self-authenticates as the very Word of God Himself. It is 'inspired by God' (2 Timothy 3:16)—that is, breathed out by the Holy Spirit of God.

There is no book like the Bible as this book alone reveals the Maker's instructions for a happy life, a happy death and a happy eternity. This is so because the Bible points us to the Lord Jesus Christ, God's Son and the only Saviour of sinners. The written Word and the incarnate Word are one. The 'sacred writings' were given by God 'to instruct you for salvation through faith in Christ Jesus' (2 Timothy 3:15).

The Bible, from Genesis 1:1 to Revelation 22:21, consists of sixty-six individual books. Interestingly, it begins in a garden and ends in a garden. It begins in the Garden of Eden and ends in the Garden City of the New Jerusalem. In between, it unfolds how Paradise was lost, and how Paradise is and will yet be restored by the grace of God in Christ, and how we may gain a place in the future Paradise.

The Bible is a vast book. It may seem overwhelming. It can be easy not to see the wood for the trees. This is why the following pages have been written. They will give you an overview of the Bible. If you like, they are the picture on the box of a thousand-piece jigsaw. They will enable you to see where each individual piece fits in with the whole.

They will help you to travel the main highway of the Bible and see its overall thrust.

Come now then and travel through the Bible, taking the main road, not the side roads. We are about to embark on a journey with God. We are about to embark on a Christian journey through the Book of books.

Timothy Cross
Cardiff
Wales

Adam and Eve

Chapter 1

The origins of the universe

The Bible opens with the majestic statement and assertion that, 'In the beginning God created the heavens and the earth (Genesis 1:1). Why is the universe here at all? Why is there something rather than nothing? The Bible alone gives us the true explanation. Almighty God created the universe. God alone was there at the beginning of history, and thus He alone can tell us how the universe came into being. God created it out of nothing. Genesis—the book of origins—reveals that He spoke it into existence, taking just six days to do so. He is, after all, Almighty God.

> For He spoke, and it came to be; He commanded, and it stood forth (Psalm 33:9).

> By faith we understand that the world was created by the word of God, so that what is seen was made out of things which do not appear (Hebrews 11:3).

The origins of humanity

Amazingly, according to the Bible, the crown of God's creation was ... little old you and me. Genesis 1:26 reveals that, on the sixth day of creation, there was a special consultation within the divine trinity of persons: 'Then God said, "Let us make man in our image."' Verse 27 then records: 'So God created man in His own image, in the image of God He created him; male and female He created them.' This verse speaks volumes about our human identity. Why are human beings special? What distinguishes us from dogs and cats? Our distinguishing mark is that we are made in the image of God. We are designed for a relationship with our Maker. We find our ultimate fulfilment by being in fellowship with God, knowing, loving, adoring and depending on Him. The *Shorter Catechism*[1] is right when it begins: 'What is the chief end of man? Man's chief end is to glorify God and to enjoy Him for ever.'

> *We are designed for a relationship with our Maker.*

As an important aside, we note from Genesis that God's design for humanity includes a distinction of gender: 'male and female He created them'. This was endorsed by the Lord Jesus in a dispute with the Pharisees. He said, 'Have you not read that He who made them from the beginning made them male and female' (Matthew 19:4). The Bible teaches the complementarity of the gender. Men and women complement each other both physically, emotionally and spiritually. To go against this grain, and blur the distinction between male and female—as promulgated by homosexuality and transexuality—is to go against the Creator's grain and created order, and will reap what it sows.

Created by God for God

When we turn to Genesis 2, we are given more details

and specifics about our creation. There we see that our first ancestor was created by a direct act of God Himself. Genesis 2:7 records how, 'the LORD God formed man of dust from the ground, and breathed into his nostrils the breath of life; and man became a living being'. Interestingly, the Hebrew word for ground is Adamah, hence 'Adam'— the first human being. Hence also our bi-partite nature. We are one person, but we consist of body and soul, the physical and the spiritual, and one affects the other—as psychosomatic illness also informs us.

Adam lived in the most perfect conditions. He lived in Paradise. 'The LORD God planted a garden in Eden, in the east; and there He put the man whom He had formed' (Genesis 2:8). What more could Adam have ever wanted or needed? The answer is human company. Genesis 1:31 says, 'God saw everything that He had made, and behold, it was very good.' But in Genesis 2:18 we read: 'Then the LORD God said, "It is not good that the man should be alone; I will make him a helper fit for him."' The LORD God then proceeded to meet Adam's need. Putting Adam to sleep, He performed surgery on him, and created Eve out of one of Adam's ribs. He then performed the first ever marriage ceremony and brought her to Adam. Adam was amazed. This was what was lacking in his life! 'Then the man said, 'This at last is bone of my bones and flesh of my flesh; she shall be called Woman, because she was taken out of Man"' (Genesis 2:23). Here then we have the origin of human marriage. Monogamous, heterosexual marriage is not so much a good idea but God's idea. It originated in Paradise. 'Therefore a man leaves his father and his mother and cleaves to his wife, and they become one flesh' (Genesis 2:24). Marriage is a divine institution—a creation ordinance.

Where did it all go wrong?

So, Adam and Eve lived in bliss. They lived in Paradise. They enjoyed happy fellowship with both God their Maker and with one another. All was harmonious. All could not have been more perfect. But the main theme of the Bible is that of Paradise Lost and Paradise Restored. The background to the Christian gospel is that of a Paradise Lost. Sin entered the world and spoiled the harmony which Adam and Eve had enjoyed. Sin caused a rift between the creature and their Creator. The consequences of this are still with us today.

The main theme of the Bible is that of Paradise Lost and Paradise Restored.

Sadly, Adam and Eve rebelled against God. Satan enticed them to eat a certain fruit which God had forbidden. No sooner had they done this than their fellowship with God was spoiled. They brought on themselves spiritual death. No sooner had they touched and bitten into the forbidden fruit than the judgment of God fell down on them, as

God had said it would. The outcome was that they were eventually banished from the Garden of Eden. The collateral damage included pain in childbirth for Eve and arduous labour for Adam, for the environment was now not so conducive. But what does all this have to do with us? Everything. We have inherited Adam's sinful nature. We are sinners by nature and practice. We too are under the judgment of God because we are Adam's descendants. He is our representative—our federal head. 'Sin came into the world through one man and death through sin, and so death [the judgment of God] spread to all men because all men sinned' (Romans 5:12). The history of Adam and Eve therefore is mostly a tragic one ... but not quite.

The promise of redemption

The Bible reveals a God who is merciful as well as just. When all seemed lost, He promised a Redeemer—one who would 'bruise your [Satan's] head' (Genesis 3:15)—crush the one who had catalysed the sin and consequent misery. The Redeemer would undo the consequences of our fall into sin and put things right! Genesis 3:15 therefore is the first gospel promise of the Bible. The Old Testament is one great unfolding of this promise. Little by little God added to it, until 'when the time had fully come, God sent forth His Son, born of woman, born under the law, to redeem those who were under the law, so that we might receive adoption as sons' (Galatians 4:4–5).

Adam evidently believed and embraced God's promise of a Redeemer. He was saved on account of the Christ to come. The LORD God sacrificed an animal to atone for his and his wife's sins. 'The LORD God made for Adam and for his wife garments of skins, and clothed them' (Genesis 3:21). The grace of God covered their sin and shame. It was a pre-figuration of the atonement Christ Himself was to make in the fullness of time.

Their history is our history. We are inextricably involved.

Adam and Eve. Their story is our story. Their history is our history. We are inextricably involved. Theirs was the sin, but God's was the intervening grace of salvation. The Bible teaches that Adam was a type of the Christ who was to come—a type of Jesus, 'the last Adam' (1 Corinthians 15:45). The Bible makes much of the contrast between these two representative men or 'Adams'. It says, 'For by one man's disobedience many will be made sinners, so by one man's obedience many will be made righteous' (Romans 5:19). Adam disobeyed God, but Christ 'became obedient unto death, even death on a cross' (Philippians 2:8). Adam's sin brought calamity on all his descendants—on us all. Christ's obedience, however—His sinless life and sacrificial death—brings salvation on all who believe in Him—the forgiveness of sins, a righteous status and restored fellowship with God. We are all descendants from

Adam through natural generation. But it is only by grace that we belong to the last, or second Adam. All are related to Adam by natural descent, but not all belong to Christ by supernatural and saving grace. You are 'in Adam', but are you 'in Christ'? If not, the invitation of the gospel still avails for you. 'Believe in the Lord Jesus and you will be saved' (Acts 16:31).

> Oh loving wisdom of our God
> When all was sin and shame
> A Second Adam to the fight
> And to the rescue came.
> (John Henry Newman 1801–1890)

Noah and the
Great Flood
2300 BC

In Hebrews 11:7 we read: 'By faith Noah, being warned by God concerning events as yet unseen, took heed and constructed an ark for the saving of his household ...' The 'events as yet unseen' here refer to a great flood sent by God to destroy all life on earth.

A downward spiral

We saw in our previous chapter how sin entered the world. 'Sin is any want of conformity unto or transgression of the law of God' (*Shorter Catechism*[1]). Sin is rebellion against God. Sin, by its nature, if unchecked, gets worse and worse. In the generations after Adam, as the population on earth grew, so rebellion against God grew. So much was this so that in Noah's day, Almighty God intervened and took action. He determined that a new start was necessary for His world. Spiritually, the world was a write-off. Scripture records:

> The LORD saw that the wickedness of man was great in the earth, and that every imagination of the thoughts of his heart was only evil continually. And the LORD was sorry that He had made man on the earth, and it grieved Him to His heart. So the LORD said, 'I will blot out man whom I have created from the face of the ground, man and beast and creeping things and birds of the air, for I am sorry that I have made them' (Genesis 6:5–7).

The universal Flood

How did God destroy all life on earth? He did so by sending a universal flood. Scripture records how, 'the fountains of the great deep burst forth, and the windows of the heavens were opened. And the rain fell upon the earth forty days and forty nights' (Genesis 7:11, 12). God had previously revealed His plans to Noah, so that he could take action, saying, 'For in seven days I will send rain upon the earth forty days and forty nights, and every living thing that I have made I will blot out from the face of the ground' (Genesis 7:4).

Noah and the Ark

There was one godly man on the earth. His name was Noah.

All life was thus to be destroyed. God had almost written it off ... but not quite. There was one godly man on the earth. His name was Noah. 'Noah found favour in the eyes of the LORD' (Genesis 6:8). Amid a very ungodly world, rebelling against God, 'Noah was a righteous man, blameless in his generation; Noah walked with God' (Genesis 6:9). What a testimony! And so, God revealed His plans to Noah—His plans both to 'bring a flood of waters upon the earth, to destroy all flesh in which is the breath of life' (Genesis 6:17) and also a way of escape from His devastating judgment. Noah was instructed to build an ark! 'Make yourself an ark of gopher wood ...' (Genesis 6:14).

Noah's ark refers to an enormous ship. 'The ark was built to float, on the lines of a barge. It was huge—about half the length of an Atlantic liner—approximately 450ft/137metres x 45ft/14 metres' (*The Lion Encyclopaedia of the Bible*[2]). Noah was instructed to take his family and selected animals into the ark. Through this, they escaped the judgment of God when it came. The ark enabled them to rise above the waters of judgment. 'The flood continued forty days upon the earth; and the waters increased, and bore up the ark and it rose high above the earth' (Genesis 7:17). 'The ark floated on the face of the waters' (Genesis 7:18). All life was indeed destroyed—but Noah and his family were saved and spared. They were safely inside the ark. And when God had achieved His purpose, His judgment ceased, and He 'made a wind blow over the earth and the waters subsided; the fountains of the deep and the windows of the heavens were closed, the rain from the heavens was restrained, and the waters receded from the earth continually' (Genesis 8:1–3). Eventually, God commanded Noah and his family to leave the ark, and a more normal life was to begin again in a severely chastened world. God promised He would never destroy the world again in such a way, and as a pledge of His promise—His covenant—He put a glorious rainbow in the sky.

> I set my bow in the cloud and it shall be a sign of the covenant between me and the earth ... the

waters shall never again become a flood to destroy all flesh (Genesis 9:13, 15).

A parable of the Gospel

The story of Noah is plain, sober history. It is both written in the Bible and confirmed by extra-biblical

Jesus is our ark of refuge.

archaeology. But the story of Noah is also a microcosm of the main message of the Bible, for it is a parable of the gospel of Christ. We all deserve the judgment of God because we have all sinned against God. But there is a way of escape—a way which God Himself has provided. Jesus is our ark of refuge. It is His death on the cross which averts the wrath of God from us. It is His death which saves us from the condemnation we deserve. 'Jesus ... delivers us from the wrath to come' (1 Thessalonians 1:10). 'He is the propitiation or our sins' (1 John 2:2 NKJV). He is the one who turns aside the wrath of God due to us, for on the cross of Calvary He endured the wrath of God to save us from it:

> The tempest's awful voice was heard
> O Christ it broke on Thee!
> Thy open bosom was my ward
> It braved the storm for me
> Thy form was scarred, Thy visage marred
> Now cloudless peace for me.
> (Anne R Cousin 1824–1906)

The rainbow promise of God in the Bible is that, 'There

is therefore now no condemnation for those who are in Christ Jesus' (Romans 8:1).

Days of apathy

Sadly, the days of Noah seem to mirror our own. A universal flood had never occurred before Noah's day. People could not comprehend or did not believe that such a happening would or could occur. So, they went on living life as normal, oblivious to the danger ahead, and perhaps amused to see Noah building an ark on dry land. Jesus said that this depicts our world today. He is coming back to judge the world. We should heed and take action … but people carry on as if the judgment of God will never happen. The response to the gospel—God's provision of salvation—in the West is characterised mainly by apathy rather than hostility. The matters of this life take priority. Jesus said:

> As were the days of Noah, so will be the coming of the Son of man. For as in those days before the flood they were eating and drinking, marrying and giving in marriage, until the day when Noah entered the ark, and they did not know until the flood came and swept them all away, so will be the coming of the Son of man (Matthew 24:37–39).

Food, drink and marriage are, of course, good gifts of God. But there is another dimension to life. There is a God with whom we must get right if all is to be eternally well with us.

Preachers: God's watchmen

There is a God with whom we must get right if all is to be eternally well with us.

God ordains gospel preachers to point people to the way of salvation—to point people to Christ who is the only Saviour. The preacher is not responsible for the response to his message, be it either apathy or hostility. But a preacher is called to preach Christ faithfully.

A gospel preacher is to be like Noah—walking with God, pointing others to the way of salvation, but leaving the outcome to God.

> If He did not spare the ancient world, but preserved Noah, a herald of righteousness, with seven other persons when He brought a flood upon the world of the ungodly ... then the Lord knows how to rescue the godly from trial ... (2 Peter 2:5, 9).

Noah preached but those around him, to their detriment, failed to respond. Noah was 'a herald of righteousness'—he urged people to get right with God before it was too late. The gospel preacher today is called to do the same. He is called to urge sinners to believe in Jesus and so get right with God while they may—before it is too late; before His final judgment falls. The Bible says, 'every one who calls upon the name of the Lord will be saved' (Romans 10:13). The Bible says, 'Behold, now is the acceptable time; behold, now is the day of salvation' (2 Corinthians 6:2).

The Patriarchs—
Abraham, Isaac,
Jacob and Joseph
2000 BC

The majority of the chapters in Genesis, the first book of the Bible, are given over to the biographies of four men—Abraham, Isaac, Jacob and Joseph—and God's dealings with them. These four men are known as the Patriarchs—the founding fathers of the Hebrew race. They all played their part in God's unfolding plan of redemption, to save a people for Himself and His glory out of this fallen world.

Abraham

Sin being what it is, the world of Abraham's day was stuck in ignorance of the one true God and had sunk in idolatry. When Abraham—or Abram as he was initially known—was 75 years old, the living God revealed Himself sovereignly and particularly to him and called him to make a break with his father's house and go to what we now know as the land of Israel. Despite Abram's wife being both childless and well passed child-bearing age, God promised him, 'I will make of you a great nation ...' (Genesis 12:2), and descendants as many as the millions of stars in the sky (see Genesis 15:5). Accordingly, God then changed Abram's name to Abraham. The name Abram means 'exalted father', but the name Abraham means 'father of a multitude'. The reason for God's promise and intervention was simple. It was 'to be God to you and to your descendants after you' (Genesis 17:7). God's plan was gradually to bring back the fellowship enjoyed between creature and Creator in Eden before the fall.

Abraham believed God's promise, for Scripture says, 'And he believed the Lord and he reckoned it to him as righteousness' (Genesis 15:6). Humanly, the promise of God seemed incredible, considering the age and stage of both Abraham and Sarah, his wife. But Abraham took God at His word.

> In hope he believed against hope, that he should become the father of many nations; as he had been told, 'So shall your descendants be'. He did not weaken in faith when he considered his own body, which was as good as dead because he was about a hundred years old, or when he considered the barrenness of Sarah's womb. No distrust made him waver concerning the promise of God, but he grew strong in his faith as he gave glory to God, fully convinced that God was able to do what had promised (Romans 4:18–20).

THE FATHER OF THE FAITHFUL

It is Abraham's steadfast faith in God's promise—a faith that was well founded, for God did eventually give him a son and a multitude of descendants, namely the nation of Israel—that has made him go down in sacred history as 'the father of the faithful' (see Romans 4:11). Christians today

Christians today are actually saved in the same way that Abraham was—by believing the promise of God.

are actually saved in the same way that Abraham was—by believing the promise of God.

The words, 'it was reckoned to him', were written not for his sake alone, but for ours also. It will be reckoned to us who believe in Him that raised from the dead Jesus our Lord, who was put to death for our trespasses and raised for our justification (Romans 4:23–25).

God promised Abraham descendants. And this promise was fulfilled. The nation of Israel traces its physical ancestry to Abraham. Christians however—whether they be Jew or Gentile –in sharing the faith of Abraham, are described in the Bible as his spiritual descendants. Hence Paul affirmed in Galatians 3:29: 'If you are Christ's, then you are Abraham's offspring, heirs according to promise', and, 'So you see that it is men of faith who are the sons of Abraham' (Galatians 3:7).

God's promise to Abraham was very expansive. Blessing to the whole human race would come through one of his future descendants, God affirmed: 'In you all the families of the earth will be blessed' (Genesis 12:3, margin). The promise was an embryonic gospel promise, pointing to the Christ to come. 'And the scripture, foreseeing that God would justify the Gentiles by faith, preached the gospel beforehand to Abraham, saying "In you shall all the nations be blessed"'(Galatians 3:8). The reference refers to God's on-going promise of a Redeemer who would come and undo the ravages caused by sin and Satan. The reference thus refers to

From an old man called Abraham, the Saviour of the world eventually came.

the Lord Jesus Christ. The two testaments of the Bible are joined by the theme of promise and fulfilment—a fulfilment in Christ. The New Testament begins with: 'The book of the genealogy of Jesus Christ, the Son of David, the Son of Abraham' (Matthew 1:1). Through Christ all the families of the earth are truly blessed, as He is a universal Saviour— 'We know that this is indeed the Saviour of the world' (John 4:42).

So, from little insignificant acorns, great oak trees grow. From an old man called Abraham, the Saviour of the world eventually came. God moves in a mysterious way, His wonders to perform. Abraham was not perfect. Scripture is candid about his faults as well as his faith. But God chose him, God entered into a covenant with him, and God worked wonders through him. Abraham has gone down in history as 'the friend of God' (James 2:23). Abraham's age, frailties and flaws notwithstanding, there could be no better epithet.

The God of Abraham praise
Who reigns enthroned above
Ancient of everlasting days
And God of love
Jehovah! Great IAM
By earth and heaven confessed;
I bow and bless the sacred Name
For ever blessed
(Thomas Olivers 1725–99)

Isaac

Abraham's son, Isaac, comes over as a quiet man, somewhat overshadowed by his father Abraham and his son Jacob. Isaac, however, was a miracle child. As intimated, Sarah, his mother, had never had children and was now well beyond the years of childbearing. 'Abraham and Sarah were old, advanced in age; it had ceased to be with Sarah after the manner of women' (Genesis 18:11). But 'Is anything too hard for the LORD?' (Genesis 18:14). The question is a rhetorical one. 'The LORD visited Sarah as He had said, and the LORD did to Sarah as He had promised. And Sarah conceived and bore Abraham a son in his old age ...' (Genesis 21:1–2). The name Isaac means 'laughter'. It expressed the 'holy laughter' Sarah felt at the amazing ways of God with her.

And she said 'Who would have said to Abraham that

Sarah would suckle children? Yet I have borne him a son in his old age.' (Genesis 21:7).

A TIME OF TESTING: A TESTING TIME

Some of God's dealings with His people can seem very perplexing. Some years after Isaac's birth, God told Abraham to offer him in sacrifice. 'God tested Abraham' (Genesis 22:1). The order seemed

We too are called to trust God even when we don't understand.

irrational. If Abraham took Isaac's life, how would God's promise of a vast number of descendants be fulfilled? But Abraham obeyed. Abraham had faith in his God. We too are called to trust God even when we don't understand. Scripture says:

> By faith Abraham, when he was tested, offered up Isaac, and he who had received the promises was ready to offer up his only son, of whom it was said 'Through Isaac shall your descendants be named.' He considered that God was able to raise men even from the dead; hence, figuratively speaking, he did receive him back (Hebrews 11:17–19).

As it turned out, at the last minute, God prevented Abraham from killing Isaac. It was all a test of faith. Scripture then records how, 'Abraham went and took the ram, and offered it up as a burnt offering instead of his son' (Genesis 22:13). We have here a type of the Christ to come.

Scripture teaches that Jesus' death was a substitutionary death. His death was an 'instead of me' death. Isaac was spared. But God 'did not spare His own Son but gave Him up for us all' (Romans 8:32).

Isaac was to marry Rebekah, a maiden from Abraham's original homeland. Although Abraham was now in the promised land of Canaan, he was adamant that his son should not marry a Canaanite, no doubt fearing that this would have been a mixed marriage and a mismatch. Abraham knew the one true God. The Canaanites worshipped Baal, a false, fertility god. Isaac's marriage produced Esau and Jacob, and from the latter the twelve tribes of Israel came—God's Old Testament, covenant people. Isaac, too, knew the living God of his father, and God renewed His covenant promise to Abraham with Isaac.

> The LORD appeared to him ... and said, 'I am the God of Abraham your father; fear not, for I am with you and will bless you and multiply your descendants for my servant Abraham's sake' (Genesis 26:24).

Isaac responded in a God-fearing way. Knowing that sin has to be atoned for, 'He built an altar there and called upon the name of the LORD' (Genesis 26:25).

Jacob

Psalm 46:7 and 11 both read: 'the God of Jacob is our refuge'. This reveals that the God of the Bible is a God who loves and is merciful to sinners, for Scripture reveals that Jacob was anything but a saint. He was actually something of a scoundrel and a schemer. He tricked his older brother, Esau, out of his birthright, and thus deceitfully inherited his father's blessing. Esau was none too pleased and resolved to murder Jacob. Jacob then fled to his mother's home country to escape. While there, he had children through four different women, though his intention was just to marry Rachel, his Uncle Laban's daughter—an intention only eventually realised. Rachel had difficulties in producing children for Jacob, but eventually she gave birth to two, namely Joseph and Benjamin.

In spite of Jacob's trickery, God revealed Himself to him at a place called Bethel and there promised that, through him, many descendants would come, and even that the universal blessing promised to Abraham and Isaac would ensue. It was at Bethel that Jacob 'dreamed that there was a ladder set up on earth, and the top of it reached to heaven' (Genesis 28:12). This actually pictured and prefigured the Christ who was to come—the Lord Jesus Christ. How is the gulf between earth and heaven bridged? How is the separation between a sinful humanity and a holy God ever to be bridged? Through Christ and His reconciliatory work on the cross. 'There is one God and there is one Mediator between God and men, the man Christ Jesus' (1 Timothy 2:5). Speaking of the cross of Christ, the hymn writer wrote:

O safe and happy shelter
O refuge tried and sweet
O trysting place where heaven's love
And heaven's justice meet
As to the holy patriarch
That wondrous dream was given
So seems my Saviour's cross to me
A ladder up to heaven.
(Elizabeth Cecilia Clephane 1830–1908)

GOD HAS HIS WAY

Jacob needed taming. This, God did. Realising that his brother was about to murder him and his large family, Jacob turned to God in repentance, pleading God's covenant promise:

> *Jacob needed taming. This, God did.*

> Deliver me, I pray Thee, from the hand of my brother, from the hand of Esau ... Thou didst say, 'I will do you good, and make your descendants as the sand of the sea, which cannot be numbered for multitude' (Genesis 32:11, 12).

God answered his prayer of desperation, and turned the anger, attitude and intentions of Esau around. God subdued Jacob and brought him to faith in Himself. At a place called Peniel—meaning 'the face of God'—Jacob was to know a pre-incarnate appearance of the Lord Jesus Christ when, mysteriously, one night 'a man wrestled with him until the breaking of the day' (Genesis 32:24), eventually putting Jacob's thigh out of joint. Jacob was helpless but clung on. The 'man' though was more than a man, for Jacob said, 'I have seen God face to face and yet my life is preserved' (Genesis 32:30). In Bible times, names were very significant and bound up with the character of the person named. The wrestling incident with the man saw Jacob's name being changed from Jacob meaning 'supplanter' to Israel meaning 'one who strives with God'. The twelve tribes, which descended from Jacob's twelve children, became known collectively as 'the children of Israel'. Jacob was now both disabled and subdued, yet a changed man. His faith was now in God and not in his own guiles and wiles. At Peniel the man 'blessed him' (Genesis 32:29).

Joseph

The story of Joseph is a story of divine providence. 'God's works of providence are His most holy, wise and powerful preserving and governing all His creatures and all their actions' (*Shorter Catechism*[1]).

Joseph was the favourite son of Jacob, who bestowed honour on him by giving him a richly ornamented coat—sometimes known as 'the coat of many colours'. Joseph's brothers resented such a favouritism. Joseph also had some strange dreams, which suggested that one day he would have the rule over his brothers. This was the last straw: Joseph's brothers resolved to murder him. However, on second thoughts, they thought it wiser not to kill him but merely sell him into slavery in Egypt. This they did, and Joseph found himself in the land of Egypt, a long way from his family and home. There, in Egypt, Joseph's difficulties were compounded. He ended up being unjustly sent to jail. In jail, however, his ability to interpret dreams came to Pharaoh's attention. Joseph was brought out of jail to interpret Pharaoh's dreams. The dreams, Joseph said, were prophetic. They foretold seven years of plenty followed by seven years of famine. This being so, preparations should be made for the time of famine. Pharaoh was so pleased that he appointed Joseph to the second in command of the whole country, and Joseph was put in charge of the grain supplies.

Back home in Canaan, the famine was severe. Joseph's family there were affected by it. They heard though that grain was plentiful down in Egypt, so Joseph's brothers went to Egypt to buy grain. Unbeknown to them, their brother was now in charge there. Eventually, Joseph revealed himself to them—he had evidently changed his appearance—and Jacob and his family came down to live with Joseph in Egypt. It was a time of great rejoicing, as Jacob had been given the false impression by his sons that Joseph was dead. In the providence of God, however, Joseph saved his own people—the sons of Israel through whom God had promised to bless the world—from famine and thus extinction. The promise of God that Abraham would have myriads of descendants could not be thwarted. God was in total control. Even Joseph's brothers' cruel intentions were under His absolute sovereignty. 'When He summoned a famine on the land, and broke every staff of bread, He had sent a man ahead of them, Joseph, who was sold as a slave' (Psalm 105:16, 17).

Divine providence and God's leading and guiding can sometimes only be discerned when we look back.

Divine providence and God's leading and guiding can sometimes only be discerned when we look back. This was the case in Joseph's life. After the death of Jacob, the darker threads in Joseph's life all made sense to him. He explained to his brothers, 'As for you, you meant evil against me; but God meant it for good, to bring it about that many people should be kept alive, as they are today' (Genesis 50:20). The New Testament equivalent of this is to affirm,

> We know that in everything God works for good with those who love Him, who are called according to His purpose (Romans 8:28).

A GLIMPSE OF JESUS

In closing, don't we have to say that the story of Joseph makes us think of Jesus? There are certain parallels.

40

Joseph was rejected, humiliated and subsequently exalted. So was the Lord Jesus Christ in His death and resurrection. Joseph's rejection, however, was the cause of the saving of the nation from famine. And Jesus' crucifixion is the cause of the eternal salvation of all who put their faith in Him.

> O the depth of the riches and wisdom and knowledge of God! How unsearchable are His judgments and how inscrutable His ways! 'For who has known the mind of the Lord, or who has been His counsellor?' 'Or who has given a gift to Him that He might be repaid?' For from Him and through Him and to Him are all things. To Him be glory for ever. Amen (Romans 11:33–36).

Moses
1520 BC

Moses is the next great figure in the storyline of the Bible and the people of God. Moses is one of the towering figures of world history. Under Moses, God delivered the descendants of Abraham—through whom the Redeemer was promised—from slavery in Egypt. Under Moses, God gave His law which forged both the nation and the world. Under Moses, God gave detailed instructions for building a special tent for meeting up with Him, along with instructions about sacrifices necessary to attain and maintain fellowship with Him. Under Moses, God also led His people through the wilderness to the brink of the Promised Land.

Moses was a hundred and twenty years old when he died. He spent his first forty years in the opulence of an Egyptian court. He spent his next forty years in the wilderness, where he had a dramatic and formative encounter with the living Lord God of his fathers. And he spent his last forty years as the great deliverer and leader of God's people. Under Moses, the nation began to be forged into a theocracy—living under the rule and law of God and knowing His presence and blessing.

Formative years

In Moses' early years we clearly see the hand and providence of God at work. The descendants of Abraham had been in Egypt since Jacob and his family moved there during Joseph's prime ministership. They multiplied greatly and were then seen as a threat to Egypt. Because of this, Pharaoh took action. He enslaved the people of Israel, and 'made their lives bitter with hard service' (Exodus 1:14). When this did not have the desired effect of subjugating the people, he took drastic action and ordered every Hebrew male baby to be cast into the River Nile. Moses, therefore, humanly speaking, should not have lived. His parents, though, shielded him from a watery grave. His mother hid him for three months, and then made a basket for him and placed it on the Nile waters. In the providence of God, Pharaoh's daughter discovered baby Moses afloat, took pity on him and adopted him. Then, of all the people she asked to be Moses' nurse, she asked Moses' mother

Moses was thus, in the will and foreknowledge of God, brought up in something of a dual world.

and paid her for her labours. Moses was thus, in the will and foreknowledge of God, brought up in something of a dual world. He was well acquainted with the culture and ways of Egypt, and hence later was able to negotiate with Pharaoh concerning the people of Israel. Although we are not told, it is fairly certain, though, that his mother would have nurtured him in the ways of the God of his fathers—the God of Abraham, Isaac and Jacob, the one, true and living God. She would have told him that God had promised to send a Redeemer and that he, Moses, was, by birth, in the line of that Redeemer. This proved to be more formative in relation to Moses' thinking and outlook than anything else. Thank God for godly mothers! Moses consequently 'considered abuse suffered for the Christ greater wealth than the treasures of Egypt, for he looked to the reward' (Hebrews 11:26). Moses was born in Egypt. But his heart was with the one true God, not the gods of Egypt which surrounded him.

Moses' faults

Moses proved to be a great man, but Scripture reveals he was far from perfect. Although brought up in the Egyptian court, his heart's loyalty was with his own people—the children of Israel. When he came across an Egyptian beating a Hebrew, he took matters into his own hands and murdered the Egyptian, and hid his body in the sand. His rash and reckless action came to the ears of Pharaoh, who then sought Moses' life. Moses had no option but to flee. He ended up in Midian where he exchanged the luxuries of his privileged life in Egypt for the humility of being a shepherd in the wilderness, having married the daughter of Jethro who kept sheep. Meanwhile, his compatriots groaned under their bondage in Egypt and, at the end of their tether, cried to God. 'And God heard their groaning, and God remembered His covenant with Abraham, with Isaac and with Jacob' (Exodus 2:24). God had promised that Abraham's descendants would dwell in their own land, under His rule and knowing His blessing. And God had promised that, through them, He would bless the whole world. True to His word, He was shortly to take action to ensure that this was so, and He would utilise Moses and his background, training and character, that He had providentially forged, to execute His great plan. But first, Moses had to be commissioned.

Moses' call and commission

When Moses was going about his pastoral work in the wilderness one day, the most amazing event occurred. The LORD God appeared to him. 'The angel of the LORD appeared to him in a flame of fire out of the midst of a bush; and he looked, and lo, the bush was burning, yet it was not consumed' (Exodus 3:2). Here was a theophany. The God of Moses' fathers had appeared visibly to him. 'Moses hid his face, for he was afraid to look at God' (Exodus 3:6). Then God spoke. He said that He knew about His peoples' suffering in Egypt, and He was going to deliver them. He was going to bring them out of slavery—'bring them up out of that land to a good and broad land, a land flowing with milk and honey' (Exodus 3:8). And He would use Moses himself to facilitate this. God commanded Moses:

> Come, I will send you to Pharaoh that you may bring forth my people, the sons of Israel, out of Egypt (Exodus 3:10).

Moses felt inadequate to the task and began to make

excuses. God met him at his level and reassured him by revealing His Name to him. 'God said to Moses, "I AM WHO I AM"' (Exodus 3:14). The God of the Bible is all sufficient and

The God of the Bible is all sufficient and will be proved all sufficient for His peoples' needs.

will be proved all sufficient for His peoples' needs. Moses went back to Egypt. He confronted Pharaoh about his people. Pharaoh was stubborn. God sent ten plagues to soften his heart. Eventually, when God sent the angel of death over Egypt, killing the first-born of man and beast from that land, Pharaoh relented, and very willingly—and even frantically—released the people of Israel from their cruel bondage.

The Exodus

The killing of the first-born in Egypt was indiscriminate. But the first-born of Israel were untouched by the angel of death. Why and how? We shall see in our next chapter on the Exodus from Egypt. The Exodus from Egypt is a major milestone in the Old Testament. It was a redemption which prefigured a Greater Redemption to come. Moses was a central player in the Exodus from Egypt. Under God, Moses facilitated the Exodus and led the people to Mount Sinai, where God gave His law.

Law is central to a nation. The people though were not to keep the law to earn God's favour. No. God had redeemed them. They were already the recipients of His favour. The Ten Commandments are prefaced with the reminder, 'I am the Lord your God, who brought you out of the land of Egypt, out of the house of bondage' (Exodus 20:2). In both Testaments, salvation is all of grace, and obedience is all of gratitude. God also revealed the details of the tabernacle to Moses—a portable shrine where God would meet with them visibly. Included in the revealed details were stipulations about sacrifice. This was instituted so fellowship with Him could be maintained, and they all foreshadowed a greater sacrifice which was to come and put away sin for ever.

Moses' obituary

Moses' biography ends with the epitaph, 'And there has not arisen a prophet since in Israel like Moses, whom the LORD knew face to face' (Deuteronomy 34:10). God prepared Moses for his great life's work—rescuing him as a baby, giving him a forty-year education in the Egyptian court, yet with a godly mother. This was followed by forty years in the wilderness. And then he began. God is not in a hurry! His final forty years saw him leading the people out of slavery; giving them the law of God; and guiding them through the wilderness.

Moses, however, was not perfect. He may have even reached the end of his life unfulfilled. For his sins, God did not permit him to enter the Promised Land, but only view

Truly, the God of the Bible blesses us 'more abundantly than all that we ask or think' (Ephesians 3:20).

its glories from Mount Nebo. Moses must have been sad when God said to him, 'You shall see the land before you; but you shall not go there, into the land which I give to the people of Israel' (Deuteronomy 32:52). Yet Moses did eventually stand on the Promised Land! The New Testament records his appearing there with Christ on the Mount of Transfiguration. He appeared there in glory with the Christ, whom the Scriptures he had written foretold! Truly, the God of the Bible blesses us 'more abundantly than all that we ask or think' (Ephesians 3:20).

The Exodus
1410 BC

The Exodus from Egypt is one of the great milestones of the Bible. It was, and still is, commemorated and celebrated each year with a special Passover meal. The Exodus is the story of a great deliverance—a divine redemption which foreshadowed an even Greater Redemption to come: the redemption from the Egypt of sin which Christ was to accomplish in the fullness of time. The Exodus from Egypt had two facets to it: The Passover and The miracle at the Red Sea.

The Passover

Strange to say, but integral to the deliverance from Egypt was the slaying of an innocent lamb. God's final judgment on Pharaoh and Egypt was the killing of every first-born male. God pronounced to Moses:

> I will pass through the land of Egypt ... I will smite all the first-born in the land of Egypt, both man and beast; and on all the gods of Egypt I will execute judgments: I am the LORD (Exodus 12:12).

This judgment was indiscriminate. All the first-borns were to be smitten by the angel of death. But God revealed to Moses, and Moses revealed to the people of Israel, a way of escape.

A lamb could die in the place of the first-born. The lamb was to be slain. Its blood was to be shed and 'put ... on the two doorposts and the lintel' (Exodus 12:7) of the Israelite homes. The blood was their protection from the divine judgment passing through Egypt. It as good as said, 'judgment has already been done'. A central verse, from the mouth of God Himself, reads:

> The blood shall be a sign for you upon the houses where you are; and when I see the blood, I will pass over you, and no plague shall fall upon you to destroy you, when I smite the land of Egypt (Exodus 12:13).

And it all happened as God had foretold. The angel of death passed over Egypt and the Egyptian first-borns all died. Understandably, 'There was a great cry in Egypt' (Exodus 12:30). It brought Pharaoh to his knees and he finally relented. 'He summoned Moses and Aaron by night and said, "Rise up, go forth from among my people, both you and the people of Israel ..."' (Exodus 12:31). They were free from their cruel slavery! They would never forget it. They commemorated it each year by eating a special Passover meal, remembering how God in His mercy 'passed over the houses of the people of Israel in Egypt, when He slew the Egyptians but spared our houses' (Exodus 12:27).

Type and anti-type

When we take the Bible as a whole, we see that the Exodus from Egypt is a type of a greater reality to come: the eternal redemption accomplished by Christ. Central to the Passover was the shedding of the blood of a lamb.

And central to the believer's eternal redemption is the shedding of the precious blood of Christ at Calvary.

> For Christ our Paschal Lamb has been sacrificed (1 Corinthians 5:7).

> In Him we have redemption through His blood, the forgiveness of our trespasses, according to the riches of His grace (Ephesians 1:7).

Note well that the lamb had to die to spare the Israelites from judgment. It was a death which saved them from death. Likewise, Christ had to die to spare us from eternal judgment and He did. He is, 'the lamb of God, who takes away the sin of the world' (John 1:29). All Scripture points to Christ and the redemption that was achieved 'with the precious blood of Christ, like that of a lamb without blemish or spot' (1 Peter 1:19). In Jesus, all who believe know redemption from the wrath of God which we deserve for our sins:

In Jesus, all who believe know redemption from the wrath of God which we deserve for our sins.

> Precious, precious blood of Jesus
> Shed on Calvary
> Shed for rebels, shed for sinners
> Shed for thee!

> Precious blood that hath redeemed us
> All the price is paid

Perfect pardon now is offered
Peace is made

Precious blood whose full atonement
Makes us nigh to God
Precious blood, our way of glory
Praise and laud
(Frances Ridley Havergal 1836–1933)
The second facet of the Exodus from Egypt concerns:

The miracle at the Red Sea

The Israelites had been released from slavery, but their troubles were not yet over. Pharaoh changed his mind. Mustering his army of chariots, he went after the Israelites with a view to bringing them back to Egypt and bondage. They pursued the people of Israel as far as the Red Sea. Now there was a problem for God's people. The choice was either to drown or be conquered by the Egyptians. The people panicked with fear and said to Moses, 'Is it because there are no graves in Egypt that you have taken us away to die in the wilderness?' (Exodus 14:11). Moses, though, had faith in the LORD, and said, 'Fear not, stand firm and see the salvation of the LORD, which He will work for you today ...' (Exodus 14:13). And Moses' faith was vindicated. God commanded Moses to lift up his rod in order to part the waters of the Red Sea. And he did. God performed a miracle through Moses, driving back the waters of the sea so that Israel could cross in safety. The Israelites would never forget it. He, 'divided the Red Sea in sunder ... and made Israel pass through the midst of it' (Psalm 136:13, 14). Israel reached the other side safely. The Egyptians, though, would not give up and continued to hound Israel. God then gave a last command to Moses. The Egyptian chariot wheels clogged up in the Red Sea bed and God commanded Moses to order the sea to return to its normal flow. It did and Pharaoh and his army were drowned. The Bible's account concludes with a summary statement:

> Thus the LORD saved Israel from the hand of the Egyptians; and Israel saw the Egyptians dead upon the seashore (Exodus 14:30).

The song of salvation

How, though, did the people of Israel react to the mighty deliverance—the Exodus—which God wrought on their behalf? They did so in song. They sang a song of praise to God.

Then Moses and the people of Israel sang this song to the LORD, saying, 'I will sing to the LORD, for He has triumphed gloriously; the horse and his rider He has thrown into the sea' (Exodus 15:1). Singing, therefore, was a consequence of salvation. And this is even more the case in New Testament times. The Christian church is known for its hymns of praise. Christians have a salvation to celebrate, a Saviour to extol and a God to glorify. They do so in song, and they will yet do so in song. Revelation 15:3

tells us that in heaven, the redeemed occupants joyfully, 'Sing the song of Moses, the servant of God, and the song of the Lamb ...' (Revelation 15:3). Worthy is the Lamb who was slain!

Joshua
1410 BC

Chapter 6

Conquering and colonising the land

Almighty God had pronounced that the people of Israel's purpose and calling was to 'be to Me a kingdom of priests and a holy nation' (Exodus 19:6). They were to be God's people. They were to be a witness to the living God to the nations—'a people holy to the LORD your God' (Deuteronomy 26:19). A 'kingdom' implies a territory over which a king rules. Israel's calling was to live under the blessed rule of God in a particular territory and location: the Promised Land. It was Joshua—Moses' successor—who was assigned to lead the people into the Promised Land, the land of Canaan.

Taking up the torch

Taking over the leadership from a great man like Moses must have been a daunting task. Joshua though had already proved himself to be a man of faith in God. When twelve spies—of which he was one—were sent into Canaan on reconnaissance, the majority lost heart. There were giants in the land! Joshua though said, '... the LORD is with us; do not fear them' (Numbers 14:9). Now, before his major work, God graciously gave Joshua extra assurance and promised:

> As I was with Moses, so I will be with you. I will not fail you or forsake you. Be strong and of good courage; for you shall cause this people to inherit

the land which I swore to their fathers to give them (Joshua 1:5–6).

What more could Joshua ever need than this assurance and re-assurance of God's presence? 'The LORD your God is with you wherever you go' (Joshua 1:9). Joshua also had the Word of God. He was obliged and needed to know, love and obey this—as indeed are we. Divine sovereignty and human responsibility are not incompatible, hence Joshua 1:8:

Divine sovereignty and human responsibility are not incompatible.

This book of the law shall not depart out of your mouth, but you shall meditate on it day and night, that you may be careful to do according to all that is written in it; for then you shall make your way prosperous, and then you shall have good success.

Lest the people of Israel had doubts, God gave them a confirmatory sign that He had ordained Joshua as their leader. To enter the Promised Land they had to cross the River Jordan. Akin to the previous crossing of the Red Sea—which had gone down in folklore—God parted the waters of the Jordan so that the people could travel over into Canaan. Scripture records that this was for Joshua's benefit as much as being a practical necessity.

On that day the LORD exalted Joshua in the sight of all Israel, and they stood in awe of him as they had stood in awe of Moses, all the days of his life (Joshua 4:14).

Joshua fought the battle of Jericho

The city of Jericho was the first hurdle that Joshua and the people of Israel met when they invaded Canaan. Jericho was well-nigh impregnable—'shut up from within and from without' (Joshua 6:1). The conquest of Jericho was a miracle. Truth be told, God did it. By His power 'the wall fell down flat, so that the people went up into the city, every man straight before him, and they took the city' (Joshua 6:20). All of Jericho's inhabitants were utterly destroyed except, surprisingly, for a female named Rahab, along with her family. Rahab was a prostitute. Yet she became a transformed prostitute. She was saved from the destruction, but more importantly, she was eternally saved by the grace of God. Pagan though she was by birth, and 'far gone' in lifestyle, she came to know and trust the LORD God of Israel—the living and true God. She was enabled to see the futility and falsity of the Canaanite gods, and thus confessed to the Israelite spies sent into Canaan: 'The LORD your God is He who is God in heaven above and on earth beneath' (Joshua 2:11). So, Rahab was a trophy of grace. She receives honourable mention in Hebrews 11—the faith hall of fame:

> By faith the walls of Jericho fell down after they had been encircled for seven days. By faith Rahab

the harlot did not perish with those who were disobedient, because she had given friendly welcome to the spies (Hebrews 11:30–31).

Conquering and colonising

After the conquest of Jericho, the book of Joshua relates how, under Joshua, the land of Canaan was both conquered and colonised. It was conquered in fits and starts. There were some setbacks, and some of the inhabitants of Canaan remained. These proved to be a thorn in Israel's side and detrimental to her spiritual wellbeing—temptation and human weakness being what it is. The land was also colonised, meaning that it was divided up and distributed among the twelve tribes of Israel. Humanly, the conquest of Canaan cannot be explained. It was all 'of God'. As

Humanly, the conquest of Canaan cannot be explained.

Joshua said in later times, 'One man of you puts to flight a thousand, since it is the Lord your God who fights for you, as He promised you' (Joshua 23:10).

The closing chapters of the book of Joshua contain Joshua's rallying cry and call to the people of Israel. He exhorts them to remain faithful to the God who had given them a land in which to dwell, and He warns them of the consequences of disobedience to Him. Looking back and tracing the hand of God in his life and work, Joshua cried out:

> You have seen all that the LORD your God has done to all these nations for your sake, for it is the LORD your God who has fought for you (Joshua 23:3).
>
> Now therefore fear the LORD, and serve Him in sincerity and in faithfulness; put away the gods which your fathers served beyond the River and in Egypt, and serve the LORD (Joshua 24:14).

We see here that the ethics of the Bible are the same in both the Old and the New Testaments. The imperative is based on the indicative. That is, salvation is all of grace and works are all of gratitude. These are the consequences of being the object of God's favour. God is good. We are to respond to His goodness with gratitude, love, loyalty and obedience.

The land of Israel

God gave the children of Israel a land in which to dwell and know His special presence. The land became known as the land of Israel. The nations were steeped and sunk in idolatry. Israel was called to be different—separated and devoted to the true and living God. This was the ultimate purpose for the conquest of Canaan under Joshua. He 'gave their land as a heritage, a heritage to His people Israel' (Psalm 135:12). 'He drove out nations before them; He apportioned them for a possession and settled the tribes of Israel' (Psalm 78:55). Joshua 24:29 records that eventually, after his illustrious career, 'Joshua the son of Nun, the servant of the LORD, died'. He was only human. Interestingly, the name Joshua means 'The Lord saved'. His name was exactly the same as the Lord Jesus—Yeshua. His name gives Him away:

> You shall call His name Jesus for He will save His people from their sins (Matthew 1:21).

The name Joshua means 'The Lord saved'. His name was exactly the same as the Lord Jesus.

When Joshua met Jesus

Did you know that Joshua was privileged to have an encounter with his Greater namesake? The book of Joshua contains a Christophany—a pre-incarnate appearance of the Lord Jesus Christ.

> When Joshua was by Jericho, he lifted up his eyes and looked, and behold, a Man stood before him with his drawn sword in His hand; and Joshua went to Him and said to Him, 'Are you for us, or for our adversaries?' And He said, 'No; but as commander of the army of the LORD I have now come.' And Joshua fell on his face to the earth, and worshipped, and said to Him, 'What does my Lord bid His servant?' And the commander of the LORD's

army said to Joshua, 'Put off your shoes from your feet; for the place where you stand is holy.' And Joshua did so (Joshua 5:13–15).

Here Joshua encountered a Man who was more than just human. Here Joshua encountered the Lord Jesus Christ—an appearance of the Saviour before He took our human flesh permanently at His incarnation.

Jesus. He is the key to unlock the Bible. He is the true 'commander of the army of the Lord.' He is the Captain of our salvation and, if we belong to Him, 'we are more than conquerors through Him who loved us' (Romans 8:37).

The Judges
1300 BC

The era after Joshua and the triumph of entering and dividing the Promised Land was an era of apostasy. Sadly, after the death of Joshua, the people of Israel lapsed into a spiritual declension. In spite of being the redeemed people of God and in a covenant relationship with Him, they failed to live up to their high and privileged calling. Israel was called to be a witness to the living God, but sadly, they turned away from the living God and began to serve the false gods of the Canaanites, who lived around and about them.

The era is known as the time of the Judges. Who were the Judges? The Judges were military and spiritual leaders called and empowered by God to rescue the Israelite tribes from their enemies around them—enemies whom God had employed as a chastisement for turning away from Himself. Twelve of these Judges are mentioned in the book of Judges. The Judges therefore could be considered as a kind of saviour. They lived in dark times, but yet times not without chinks of light. The love story of Ruth is set in the time of the Judges. Key players in this drama include Boaz, who became Ruth's husband, and Ruth herself. Ruth—like Rahab in our previous chapter—was born into a pagan background and, similar to Rahab, came to know, trust and love the living God: 'the LORD, the God of Israel, under whose wings you have come to take refuge!' (Ruth 2:12). Ruth even ended up in the genealogy of the Messiah. Such are the amazing ways of the grace of God and the God of grace.

The time of the Judges saw a familiar cycle being repeated over and over again. The cycle may be summarised in four words: Sin, Servitude, Supplication and Salvation. Let us now see this from the book of Judges itself.

Sin

> The people of Israel did what was evil in the sight of the LORD and served the Baals; and they forsook the LORD, the God of their fathers, who had brought them out of the land of Egypt; they went after other gods, from among the gods of the peoples who were round about them ... (Judges 2:11–12).

The sin in question here was the sin of apostasy—turning away from the living God. It was also a case of idolatry—serving a false god. The true God is real but invisible. The false god of Baal—believed to be the god of fertility—could be seen, as it was a visible idol. The Israelites wanted good crops, so they gave into the temptation to serve Baal. Yet the Lord had commanded, 'You shall have no other gods before Me' (Exodus 20:3). Forsaking the Lord, however, had consequences!

Forsaking the Lord, however, had consequences!

68

Servitude

> So, the anger of the LORD was kindled against
> Israel, and He gave them over to plunderers, who
> plundered them; and He sold them into the power
> of their enemies round about ... the hand of the
> LORD was against them for evil (Judges 2:14, 15).

God is not apathetic towards sin. He reacts with righteous indignation when His commandments are broken. He, thus, used the nations who still dwelt in the Promised Land as a chastisement. They brought Israel into bondage again because of their sin. They brought Israel low. Behind it all, however, was the hand of God. He was being cruel to be kind. He was calling His people back to Himself. He was reminding them of their total dependence on Him. The trials of life are still designed to have this effect in the lives of God's children. 'It is good for me that I was afflicted, that I might learn Thy statutes' (Psalm 119:71). 'For the Lord disciplines him whom He loves and chastises every son whom He receives' (Hebrews 12:6). At the time of the Judges, the chastisement from the Lord is shown to have had the effect for which it was intended, for it brought God's people to their knees.

Supplication

> When the people of Israel cried to the LORD, the
> LORD raised up for them a deliverer (Judges 3:15).

God's punishment of His people gave Him their

attention back. Sometimes, we only prove the Lord's all-sufficiency when all our human props are taken away. This was often the case in the days of the Judges. Helpless against their enemies, 'the people of Israel cried to the LORD for help' (Judges 4:3). And God heard their prayers and intervened. He raised up deliverers and He wrought for the Israelites a deliverance through them.

> *Sometimes, we only prove the Lord's all-sufficiency when all our human props are taken away.*

Salvation

> Then the LORD raised up judges, who saved them out of the power of those who plundered them (Judges 2:16).

> Whenever the LORD raised up judges for them, the LORD was with the judge, and He saved them from the hand of their enemies all the days of the judge; for the LORD was moved to pity by their groaning because of those who afflicted and oppressed them (Judges 2:18).

So, the Lord mercifully intervened in response to His peoples' supplication. The book of Judges shows how He saved His people when they turned back to Him, after having turned their backs on Him. And Judges shows how the Lord employed judges—military deliverers—to bring the deliverance about.

Some of the judges are well known—Samson, Gideon and Deborah have gone down into folklore. Others, such as Shamgar and Jephthah, are not so very well known. It is noteworthy that the judges' weaknesses and frailties are recorded, as well as their strengths and courageous exploits. Samson's immorality is well known. Gideon was by nature somewhat timid and subject to doubt. 'Jephthah ... was a mighty warrior, but he was the son of a harlot' (Judges 11:1). Deborah was female in a patriarchal society. Yet God used them all to accomplish His purposes. While God never condones our sins, Christian ministry is as much today as it was then, a matter of God using imperfect human vessels to accomplish His eternal purposes of grace and glory.

Same old story

So, the times of the Judges were not exactly a golden era in the history of God's people. No sooner had a judge delivered the people from oppression, than the cycle of sin, servitude, supplication and salvation began again. The times were characterised by apostasy—they turned away from God; anger—God judged their sin; apology—at their wits' end they repented of their sin and turned back to God; action—God, through the judges, delivered his people, before the downward spiral began again.

Sadly, during the days of the judges, 'every man did what was right in his own eyes' (Judges 17:6)—not what was right in the eyes of the Lord. When God's law is rejected, lawlessness results, for the law and order of heaven is replaced by the anarchy and disorder of hell. The Judges brought a temporary deliverance. They were saviours of a sort. But they all pointed towards the need for a greater Saviour. They pointed forward to the coming Deliverer promised by God. 'He will come to Zion as Redeemer, to those in Jacob who turn from transgression, says the LORD' (Isaiah 59:20). The Deliverer eventually came. His name is Jesus, and His death on the cross brings eternal deliverance for all who put their faith in Him.

The Judges

The Monarchy—
the Reigns of
Saul, David
and Solomon
1050 BC

Chapter 8

A theocratic nation

When the people of Israel, in awe of Gideon's ability at delivering them from the threat of the Midianites, sought to make him king over them, Gideon replied, 'I will not rule over you, and my son will not rule over you; the LORD will rule over you' (Judges 8:23).

Up until the time we are shortly to consider, the people of Israel were a theocracy. That meant, in principle, they were ruled by God—though as we saw in the time of the Judges, they did not always submit and live in obedience to His rule. As a theocratic confederation of twelve tribes under God, Israel had no human ruler or government. This, though, was to change when the various judges were replaced by one king, who had a greater unifying influence.

Kingship

A monarchical government was actually foretold by God before Israel entered the Promised Land. The stipulations and duties for a king are laid down in Deuteronomy 17:14 and onwards. 'You may indeed set as king over you him whom the LORD your God will choose' (Deuteronomy 17:15). Israel, however, was always called to be a theocracy, having the king as God's vice-regent. The king was to rule in the fear of the Lord and lead the people in God's ways. He too was bound by God's Book—the law of Moses.

And when he sits on the throne of his kingdom, he shall

write for himself in a book a copy of this law ... and it shall be with him, and he shall read in it all the days of his life, that he may learn to fear the LORD his God, by keeping all the words of this law and these statutes, and doing them ((Deuteronomy 17:18, 19).

Why then, at the time we are considering, was Samuel—the last Judge and seer—so displeased when the elders of Israel came to him and said, 'Now appoint for us a king to govern us like all the nations' (1 Samuel 8:5)? The clue is in the words, 'like all the nations'. Israel's calling was not to be like the nations around them. They were called to be holy. They were called to be God's people. 'For you are a people holy to the LORD your God; the LORD your God has chosen you to be a people for His own possession, out of all the peoples that are on the face of the earth' (Deuteronomy 7:6). By way of application, it is the same with Christians today. Christians are to stand out for Christ. We are called to be non-conformists!

> *Christians are to stand out for Christ. We are called to be non-conformists!*

> Do not be conformed to this world, but be transformed by the renewal of your mind, that you may prove what is the will of God, what is good and acceptable and perfect (Romans 12:2).

Scripture records that God acceded to the peoples'

demands, even though their desire for a king was both spiritually symptomatic and socially problematic. God explained to Samuel, 'Hearken to the voice of the people in all that they say to you; for they have not rejected you, but they have rejected me from being king over them' (1 Samuel 8:7). He instructed Samuel to explain to the people the social and economic drawbacks of having a king and that they might regret ever having one –but the people were not convinced. Adamantly they persisted:

> No! But we will have a king over us, that we also may be like all the nations, and that our king may govern us and go out before us and fight our battles (1 Samuel 8:19–20).

> And the LORD said to Samuel, 'Hearken to their voice and make them a king' (1 Samuel 8:22).

And thus began a sea change—the era of Israelite kingship.

Saul—the first king

Samuel was guided by providence to anoint Saul, the son of Kish, as the first king of Israel. Anointing with oil signified being set apart by God for a specific task, whether prophet, priest or king.

> Then Samuel took a vial of oil and poured it on his head, and kissed him and said, 'Has not the LORD anointed you to be prince over His people Israel? And you shall reign over the people of the LORD and

> you will save them from the hand of their enemies
> round about' (1 Samuel 10:1).

This private anointing was then confirmed publicly:

> And all the people shouted, 'Long live the king!'
> (1 Samuel 10:24).

Saul's reign began well. He certainly looked the part. 'He was taller than any of the people from his shoulders upward' (1 Samuel 10:23), and was blessed with a victory in battle, delivering Israel from the threat of the Ammonites. In humility, Saul gave all the glory and credit to God, saying, 'today the LORD has wrought deliverance in Israel' (1 Samuel 11:13). With delight, the people of Israel, sure that they had made the right choice in choosing to have Saul as king, went to Gilgal, and Saul underwent a renewal of his kingship ceremony. What could go wrong? Sadly, much.

As time went on, Saul's reign took a downward spiral. We see him usurping the office of a priest by offering a sacrifice—the prerogative of a priest alone. We see him becoming increasingly jealous of the exploits of young David to the point of paranoia. We see him sparing King Agag, the Amalekite, and his animals, when the commandment of God was that they should be utterly destroyed. We see his military leadership failing when the Philistines attacked Israel. In desperation, Saul turned to the witch of Endor for help, dabbling in the black arts— forbidden by God. Samuel's verdict on Saul was stark:

'You have rejected the word of the Lord, and the Lord has rejected you from being king over Israel' (1 Samuel 15:26).

Samuel's prophetic words were eventually fulfilled. Saul was fatally wounded in battle against the Philistines. Rather than be killed by the hand of an idolatrous nation, he committed suicide and literally fell on his own sword. Such was the sad ending of Israel's first king.

David—Israel's greatest king

When King Saul fell away from the path of obedience to the Lord, Samuel said to him:

> Now your kingdom shall not continue; the Lord has sought out a man after His own heart; and the Lord has appointed him to be prince over His people (1 Samuel 13:14).

This man after God's own heart refers to David, who subsequently went down in history as Israel's greatest earthly king.

He chose David His servant, and took him from the sheepfolds; from tending the ewes that had young He brought him to be the shepherd of Jacob His people, of Israel His inheritance (Psalm 78:70–71). David the shepherd boy was to prove to be a great poet and musician—he was responsible for many of the Psalms in the Psalter—a great warrior and a great king.

'The Lord has sought out a man after His own heart.'

79

EARLY YEARS

It was David's early experience as a shepherd which enabled him to write one of the most famous portions of Scripture of all: Psalm 23. A shepherd's chief concern is the welfare of his sheep. David had come to know the Lord God of Israel. He was aware that he was under God's pastoral care. He could thus affirm, using a metaphor he knew, that, 'The Lᴏʀᴅ is my shepherd, I shall not want' (Psalm 23:1). His early experience as a shepherd nurtured in him both courage and faith in God. He testified to delivering his sheep from both bears and lions, and he went on to deliver the people of Israel from the intimidating Philistine giant, Goliath, employing his expertise with a sling and stone. This well-known contest was both physical and spiritual, for David said to Goliath, 'You come to me with a sword and with a spear and with a javelin; but I come to you in

David's early experience as a shepherd nurtured in him both courage and faith in God.

the name of the Lᴏʀᴅ of hosts, the God of the armies of Israel, whom you have defied' (1 Samuel 17:45). The news concerning David's victory over the Philistine giant spread abroad. Saul was still king of Israel and became intensely jealous of David's fame and the admiration and adulation given to him. He saw David as a threat. So much was this so, that Saul sought to kill him. David was a marked man and became a fugitive, though he continued to gain much support. Even the experience of being an outlaw, however, was sanctified to him. He learned to depend on God even more, and composed many Psalms during this time, for example:

> Be merciful to me, O God, be merciful to me, for in Thee my soul takes refuge; in the shadow of Thy wings I will take refuge, till the storms of destruction pass by (Psalm 57:1).

KING DAVID

After Saul and Jonathan had been killed in battle, David was crowned king, first in Judah, and once the threat of Saul's house was finally ended, over all the land of Israel.

> David was thirty years old when he began to reign, and he reigned forty years. At Hebron he reigned over Judah seven years and six months; and at Jerusalem he reigned over all Israel and Judah thirty-three years (2 Samuel 5:4–5).

JERUSALEM

A milestone in David's kingship was his capture of the city of Jerusalem, which was run by the Jebusites. This made Jerusalem the religious and political capital of Israel. With great ceremony, David brought the Ark of the Covenant from the tabernacle to Jerusalem. On the mercy seat of the Ark, God presenced Himself in a particular, localized

David became greater and greater, for the LORD, the God of hosts, was with him.

way. It was this which made Jerusalem a holy city—the city of God. Solomon—David's son and successor—eventually replaced the tent in which the Ark was located with a more permanent and greater temple building. The seat of David was thus now in Jerusalem, and it became known forever after as 'the city of David' (2 Samuel 5:9). Scripture explains David's kingship as ultimately being due to the work of God, not David's own abilities.

> David became greater and greater, for the LORD, the God of hosts, was with him (2 Samuel 5:10).

> And David perceived that the LORD had established him king over Israel, and that He had exalted his kingdom for the sake of his people Israel (2 Samuel 5:12).

THE BEST OF MEN ARE MEN AT BEST

David ruled well and won many more victories in battle. He was popular and a time of peace eventually prevailed, for 'the LORD had given him rest from all his enemies round about' (2 Samuel 7:1). Yet the best of men are men at best. David's vices, as well as his virtues, are recorded for us in Scripture. His adultery with Bathsheba is notorious. He tried to cover this up by orchestrating the killing of Uriah,

Bathsheba's husband. But he could not hide from God. He was rebuked by Nathan the prophet and subsequently smitten in conscience. His remorse and repentance are evident from Psalm 51, composed as a result of this sordid episode. David made mistakes and David sinned. Yet he always turned back to God for mercy. He was truly a man after God's own heart. He suffered the consequences of his sin. His family life became chaotic. Two of his sons—Absalom and Adonijah—both plotted against him and tried unsuccessfully to usurp his kingship. They were thwarted but caused David much turmoil.

GREAT DAVID'S GREATER SON

David's rule went down as something of a golden time. Yet this apart, he did not bring in the anticipated, glorious Kingdom of Heaven—the time of spiritual peace, prosperity and righteousness under God's special rule. He was not the promised Redeemer! God, though, promised that One of his descendants would do all this and more. Through Nathan the prophet, God foretold to David, 'I will raise up your offspring after you ... and I will establish His kingdom. He shall build a house for my name and I will establish the throne of His kingdom for ever' (2 Samuel 7: 12, 13). After David's time, Isaiah the prophet likewise foretold of a certain child who would be born:

> Of the increase of His government and of peace there will be no end, upon the throne of David, and

over His kingdom, to establish it, and to uphold it with justice and with righteousness from this time forth and for evermore (Isaiah 9:7).

Only one person fulfils these prophecies: King Jesus, great David's Greater Son. At His conception in the womb of the virgin Mary, it was said of Him:

He will be great, and will be called the Son of the Most High; and the Lord God will give to Him the throne of His father David, and He will reign over the house of Jacob for ever; and of His kingdom there will be no end (Luke 1:32–33).

It is through Christ that we enter the Kingdom of Heaven. It is through Christ that we enjoy a present salvation. It is through Christ that we will yet enjoy a perfect salvation when He comes again to reign and put all God's enemies under His feet.

It is through Christ that we will yet enjoy a perfect salvation when He comes again to reign.

Hail to the Lord's Anointed
Great David's Greater Son
Hail in the time appointed
His reign on earth begun
He comes to break oppression
To set the captive free
To take away transgression

And rule in equity

(James Montgomery 1771–1854)

Solomon—a backsliding king

Solomon—King David's successor and son—inherited a peaceful and stable kingdom from his father. This, Solomon maintained, protecting Israel's borders with a strong army and with fortresses built by forced labour. Solomon began his reign well. 1 Kings 3:3 tells us, 'Solomon loved the LORD, walking in the statues of David his father.' Sadly, this did not continue for the whole of his reign, as Scripture reveals his backsliding. When he began his reign though, on realising the immensity of his role, he prayed to God for wisdom. 'Give thy servant therefore an understanding mind to govern Thy people that I may discern between good and evil; for who is able to govern this Thy great people?' (1 Kings 3:9). Scripture then records, 'It pleased the LORD that Solomon had asked this' (1 Kings 3:10). 'And God gave Solomon wisdom and understanding beyond measure ...' (1 Kings 4:29).

THE WISDOM OF SOLOMON: THE WEALTH OF SOLOMON

It is to Solomon that we largely owe the book of Proverbs, part of the Wisdom literature of the Bible. This has many 'golden verses', such as Proverbs 3:5–6:

> Trust in the LORD with all your heart, and do not rely on your own insight. In all your ways acknowledge Him, and He will make straight your paths.

God answered Solomon's prayer for wisdom, and because he had asked aright, God also rewarded him with the promise of riches and honour. This promise was fulfilled in due time. Eventually, 'King Solomon excelled all the kings of the earth in riches and in wisdom' (1 Kings 10:23). Under Solomon, the nation of Israel thrived economically and materially. He had a fleet of ships and these traded with other nations. 'For the king had a fleet of ships of Tarshish at sea with the fleet of Hiram. Once every three years the fleet of ships of Tarshish used to come bringing gold, silver, ivory, apes and peacocks'(1 Kings 10:22). 'Now the weight of gold that came to Solomon in one year was six hundred and sixty-six talents of gold' (1 Kings 10:14).

Materially, the nation of Israel never reached the heights of Solomon's reign, before or since. Under Solomon, the economy thrived.

THE TEMPLE AT JERUSALEM

Perhaps the standout feature of Solomon's reign was his building of the temple in Jerusalem, to replace the tent of meeting—the tabernacle—with a more solid, permanent structure. The building materials and labourers for the temple were from Hiram, the king of Tyre, in exchange for wheat and beaten oil. The temple took seven years to build. The day came for the Ark of the Covenant to be brought into it. The men of Israel assembled and, 'the glory of the

We saw in our last chapter that the main feat of King Solomon's reign was his building of the temple at Jerusalem. This was finished in 960 BC and stood until 587 BC, when it was destroyed by the Babylonians, under king Nebuchadnezzar, after they captured Jerusalem. When the Jews returned from exile in Babylon in 538 BC, Zerubbabel laid the foundations for a new temple. This temple was built in 'fits and starts', but through the encouragement of Haggai and Zechariah, the prophets, it was completed in 515 BC. It stood for five hundred years. In 19 BC, King Herod the Great began extensive renovations of this temple. The main edifice for this work was finished in 9 BC, yet the work was still on-going during the time of Christ. In AD 70 the temple at Jerusalem was destroyed by the Romans—as Christ prophesied it would be—and has never been rebuilt.

The house of God

The permanent building of the temple in Solomon's time was modelled on the portable building of the tabernacle—the tent of meeting—in Moses' time. Both were the special dwelling place of God Himself. The people of Israel were supremely blessed by having the special presence of God in their midst. In both buildings, the omnipresent, invisible God manifested His presence in a visible, localized, particular way. God commanded Moses, 'Let them make me a sanctuary, that I may dwell in their midst' (Exodus 25:8), and proceeded to give the architectural plans for the tabernacle. Then, sure enough, once completed, 'The cloud covered the tent of meeting, and the glory of the Lord filled the tabernacle' (Exodus 40:34). Similarly, once Solomon's temple was constructed, 'When the priests came out of the holy place, a cloud filled the house of the Lord, so that the priests could not stand to minister because of the cloud; for the glory of the Lord filled the house of the Lord' (1 Kings 8:10–11). The temple was literally 'the house of God', where God's presence was seen and felt. It was also a place of sacrifice, for fellowship with such a holy God could only be enjoyed once atonement for sin had been made, and '… without the shedding of blood there is no forgiveness of sins' (Hebrews 9:22).

> *The temple was literally 'the house of God', where God's presence was seen and felt.*

The design of the temple

The design of the temple was quite simple. It had an outer court and a room known as the holy place. The holy place was subdivided into the holy of holies in which was the Ark of the Covenant—a box containing the ten commandments. Two carved cherubim overshadowed the Ark of the Covenant, and this was known as the 'mercy seat'. It was here that God manifested Himself. Access

God Himself will be with them; He will wipe away every tear from their eyes and death shall be no more, neither shall there be mourning nor crying nor pain any more, for the former things have passed away.

In glory, the temple and other means of grace will be needed no more. Hence, John records that there,

I saw no temple in the city, for its temple is the Lord God the Almighty and the Lamb. And the city has no need of sun or moon to shine upon it, for the glory of God is its light and its lamp is the Lamb (Revelation 21:22–23).

For the Christian, the best is yet to be!

The Divided Kingdom
930 BC

We have seen that King Solomon ended his days in apostasy. But after his death, matters took an even greater downturn. After King Solomon, the people of God lost their unity and were divided into the ten tribes of Israel in the north, and the two tribes of Judah in the south. The following years were characterised by disunity, idolatry, wars, disputes and disruptions when civil war broke out between the two divisions which led to their eventual defeat by foreign powers and eventual exile.

The ten tribes of Israel were eventually conquered by the Assyrians who deported them to Assyria. The king of Assyria also deported people from various nations and placed them in the cities of Samaria in northern Israel. Those in the north of Israel were thus a mixed race and not pure Jews. This explains the contempt for Samaritans in the New Testament. The two tribes of Judah, however, also did not escape. Their territory was conquered by the Babylonians. Judah was eventually exiled to Babylon, yet, in the sovereign will of God, returned to the Promised Land after seventy years. The descendants of Abraham were chastised but not eradicated. God ensured that this was so as He had promised that the Messiah would come through Abraham's lineage.

> To them belong the Patriarchs, and of their race, according to the flesh is the Christ, who is God over all, blessed for ever. Amen (Romans 9:5, KJV).

What caused it?

How was it that the people of God became divided into two kingdoms, Israel in the north and Judah in the south? The trigger was Solomon's son Rehoboam, who inherited his father's throne. Rehoboam was both unwise and ill-advised. He treated his subjects harshly, causing them to rebel against his rule. The cry then went up, 'What portion have we in David? We have no inheritance in the son of Jesse. To your tents, O Israel! Look now to your own house, David' (1 Kings 12:16).

Rehoboam still reigned in Jerusalem, but only over two tribes. The other ten tribes made Jeroboam king. Jeroboam is described in 1 Kings 11:28 as, 'very able' and 'industrious'. He was evidently a natural leader. There were now, though, two kingdoms in the land of Israel, ruled by two different kings. King Jeroboam, fearing that his subjects would go to the temple in Jerusalem to offer sacrifices and in so doing, return to Rehoboam's kingship, took matters into his own hands. He made two calves of gold and decreed to his subjects, 'You have gone up to Jerusalem long enough. Behold your gods, O Israel, who brought you up out of the land of Egypt. And he set one in Bethel, and the other he put in Dan' (1 Kings 12:28–29). The editorial comment then states: 'And this thing became a sin ...' (1 Kings 12:30).

Idolatry

Jeroboam, in his action, was legislating idolatry. He even

instituted a rival priesthood, not of God, to rival the priesthood in Jerusalem. Israel, though, followed him. Other kings in his succession proved to do nothing to stop the idolatry and apostasy. Jeroboam's leadership and example went down in the history of Israel as notorious and the first of many who 'did what was evil in the sight of the LORD, and walked in the way of Jeroboam and in his sin which he made Israel to sin' (1 Kings 15:34).

The divided kingdom therefore refers to the time of a breaking away from David and his successors' rule—a division into Israel in the north and Judah in the south. The division was never actually healed. It was a time of great political instability, and yet a time totally foreseen and revealed beforehand by God Himself to the prophet Ahijah.

As prophesied

Ahijah met Jeroboam, the would-be king of Israel, and predicted the following in what turned out to be detailed accuracy:

> Then Ahijah laid hold of the new garment that was on him and tore it into twelve pieces. And he said to Jeroboam, 'Take for yourself ten pieces; for thus says the LORD, the God of Israel, "Behold, I am about to tear the kingdom from the hand of Solomon, and will give you ten tribes, (but he shall have one tribe, for the sake of my servant David and for the sake

of Jerusalem, the city which I have chosen out of all the tribes of Israel), because he has forsaken Me ..."' (1 Kings 11:30 onwards).

Ahijah thus gave an enacted prophecy. He used a visual aid! And the prophecy was fulfilled to the letter. The people of God were, as it were, torn into two.

Like king, like people, the nation turned further and further away from the living God.

The life and times of Israel during the divided kingdom was, on the whole, characterised by apostasy. Like king, like people, the nation turned further and further away from the living God. Yet this was not wholly so. God 'did not leave Himself without witness ...' (Acts 14:17), as we see from the following examples:

Elijah

Elijah the prophet stood boldly for the living God in a time of great apostasy, under King Ahab and his wicked wife Jezebel. He issued a challenge on Mount Carmel: 'If the LORD is God, follow Him, but if Baal, then follow him' (1 Kings 18:21). He proceeded to build an altar on Mount Carmel and said to the false prophets of Baal, 'You call on the name of your god and I will call on the name of the LORD; and the God who answers by fire, he is God' (1 Kings 18:24). The futility of calling on Baal was eventually revealed, but in answer to Elijah's prayer, 'the fire of the LORD fell, and consumed the burnt offering' (1 Kings 18:38). The people were awestruck and responded, 'The LORD, He is God; the LORD, He is God' (1 Kings 18:39). Yes, they were idolatrous days, but Elijah was 'very jealous for the LORD, the God of hosts, for the people of Israel ... [had] ... forsaken Thy covenant...' (1 Kings 19:10).

Asa, Jehoshaphat, Hezekiah and Josiah

King Asa of Judah 'did what was right in the eyes of the LORD, as David his father had done' (1 Kings 15:11), and made certain reforms in Judah, bringing it more in-line with the Law of Moses. Asa was succeeded by his son Jehoshaphat. Jehoshaphat was not perfect, but Scripture says of him, 'He walked in all the way of Asa his father; he did not turn aside from it; doing what was right in the eyes of the LORD' (1 Kings 22:43).

When the Assyrians were successfully invading Israel in the north, Hezekiah, king of Judah, feared that they would share their fate and be overcome. Hezekiah had a zeal for the living God. He turned to God in prayer and repentance. He knew that king Sennacherib of Assyria was mighty, *Hezekiah had a zeal for the living God.* but he also knew that the living God was all-mighty. He thus prayed, 'So now, O LORD our God, save us from his hand, that all the kingdoms of the earth may know that

103

Thou alone art the LORD' (Isaiah 37:20). God heard and answered his prayer. The Assyrian threat was completely nullified in a way which could only be explained as an act of God: 'That night the angel of the LORD went forth and slew a hundred and eighty-five thousand in the camp of the Assyrians (2 Kings 19:35).

During the reign of Josiah, king of Judah, a great reformation and even revival occurred. It was a case of 'back to the Bible'. During temple renovations, the written Word of God was unearthed and re-discovered. Reforms in-line with the Word of God were wrought. 'When the king heard the words of the book of the law, he rent his clothes' (2 Kings 22:11). A mini reformation and revival ensued. Idols were burnt. 'Josiah put away the mediums and the wizards and the teraphim and the idols and all the abominations that were seen in the land of Judah and in Jerusalem' (2 Kings 23:24). And on a positive note:

> The king commanded all the people, 'Keep the Passover to the LORD your God, as it is written in this book of the covenant.' For no such Passover had been kept since the days of the judges (1 Kings 23:21–22).

Josiah was reminding his subjects that they were the people of God and called to be the people of God. God was their redeemer. He was the only God. He is the God of the covenant. They were obliged to love, worship, serve and obey Him.

So, the days of the divided kingdom were not wholly bad. The kings mentioned above though were sadly exceptions to the general rule. The majority of kings were corrupt. The days were mainly degenerate, and this led to the exiles of Israel in Assyria and Judah in Babylon. How they longed for God's King—the Messiah—to come. Isaiah looked forward to the time ahead and prophesied, 'Your eyes will see the king in His beauty; they will behold a land that stretches afar' (Isaiah 33:17). God's King would put things right. God's King would surely bring in the blessed Kingdom of God, with His redeemed subjects living under His rule and knowing His blessing...

How they longed for God's King—the Messiah—to come.

The divided kingdom resulted in the end of the northern kingdom. It perished after the Assyrian conquest—but the purposes of God would yet continue through Judah. They were dark days. During these days God raised up prophets—He raised up spokesmen for Himself. To these we will turn in our next chapter of God's dealings with His people.

The Prophets

The prophetic office came into especial prominence during the time of the divided kingdom of our previous chapter—although the role of prophet went back centuries before this. Moses' epitaph reads, 'And there has not arisen a prophet since in Israel like Moses, whom the LORD knew face to face' (Deuteronomy 34:10). When God initially called Moses, he began to make excuses and said that speaking was not his strong point. Scripture then records:

> Then the LORD said to him, 'Who has made man's mouth? Who makes him dumb or deaf ...? Is it not I, the LORD? Now therefore go, and I will be with your mouth and teach you what you shall speak' (Exodus 4:11–12).

The office of the prophets

Who then were the prophets who prophesied to Israel and Judah both before, during and after her exile and return to the Promised Land? Simply, the prophets were divine spokesmen. They were mouthpieces for the Almighty. They were called by God to deliver a message from God. They proclaimed the Word of God to the people and circumstances of their day. Their message, therefore, was not their own but God's. Many times, we read the 'Thus says the LORD', or 'The Word of the LORD came' prophetic formula prefacing the messages of the prophets which have been compiled in the Old Testament. In Amos 3:6, for instance we read, 'Thus says the Lᴏʀᴅ: "For three transgressions of Israel, and for four, I will not revoke the punishment."' And Joel 1:1 reads: 'The word of the Lᴏʀᴅ that came to Joel, the son of Pethuel.'

How the prophets actually came to be in the divine counsel is not really disclosed, neither is the way that they received God's message to pass on. But that they were men of God with a message from God is evident and self-authenticating. It is also evident that their individual personalities were not over-ridden or by-passed; yet mysteriously, God spoke through them, demanding and commanding attention.

> No prophecy ever came by the impulse of man, but men moved by the Holy Spirit spoke from God (2 Peter 1:21).

> Surely the Lord God does nothing without revealing His secret to His servants the prophets. The lion has roared; who will not fear? The Lord God has spoken; who can but prophesy? (Amos 3:7–8).

The message of the prophets

The prophets of Israel were both forth-tellers and foretellers—speakers and seers. In speaking the Word of God to their own generation, their message was both negative and positive. Negatively, they condemned the idolatry and apostasy which were the prevailing sins of their day. Positively they urged the people to return to the Lord their God—the God of their fathers; the God who had redeemed them; the God who had entered into a covenant with them. The prophets were thus forth-tellers. The nub of their message was a repentance and a return to the Lord God.

The prophets were also foretellers. Prediction was part of their message as well as condemnation. They were in the counsel of the eternal God—the One 'declaring the end from the beginning and from ancient times things not yet done, saying, "My counsel shall stand, and I will accomplish all my purpose"' (Isaiah 46:10). The prophets were, therefore, able to foretell events such as the exile, the return from exile and even the details concerning the coming Messiah, as all of these were already known to God and in His mind and plan. Their prophecy was, at times, history written in advance—yet they were no mere soothsayers. There was a purpose and point to everything they said.

The touchstone of prophetic truth was its fulfilment.

The touchstone of prophetic truth was its fulfilment. This distinguished whether a prophet was divinely appointed or self-appointed. False prophets were not unknown. The people who lived in Bible times were as equally sceptical and some were as equally gullible as many in our day. God therefore gave a 'prophetic test'. This is contained in Deuteronomy 18:21–22:

And if you say in your heart, 'How may we know
the word which the Lord has not spoken?'—when a
prophet speaks in the name of the LORD, if the word
does not come to pass or come true, that is a word
which the LORD has not spoken, the prophet has
spoken presumptuously, you need not be afraid of
him.

What was the broad message of the prophets of Israel?

The prophets condemned idolatry and contrasted the
worship of idols with knowing the one, true God. 'To
whom then will you liken God, or what likeness compare
with Him? The idol! A workman casts it and a goldsmith
overlays it with gold, and casts for it silver chains' (Isaiah
40:18–19). Idols were powerless to hear prayer and give
help, for they were dead. Hence, God said through the
prophet Hosea, 'O Ephraim, what have I to do with idols?
It is I who answer and look after you. I am like an evergreen
cypress, from me comes your fruit' (Hosea 14:8). Hence
also, God's words through Jeremiah the prophet: 'The
instruction of idols is but wood! ... They are the work of the
craftsman and of the hands of the goldsmith; ... they are
all the work of skilled men. But the LORD is the true God;
He is the living God and the everlasting King' (Jeremiah
10:8, 9, 10).

The prophets condemned the apostasy of their day,

and pointed out its folly, for true joy, they said, was found in the Lord alone. 'My people have committed

True joy, they said, was found in the Lord alone.

two evils: they have forsaken ME, the fountain of living waters, and hewed out cisterns for themselves, broken cisterns that can hold no water' (Jeremiah 2:13).

The prophets of Israel preached repentance. That is, they exhorted the people to return to the Lord from whom they had turned aside.

> 'Yet even now' says the LORD, 'return to me with all your heart, with fasting, with weeping, and with mourning; and rend your hearts and not your garments.' Return to the LORD your God, for He is gracious and merciful, slow to anger, and abounding in steadfast love and repents of evil (Joel 2:12–13).

The prophets condemned the social corruption and exploitation of their day, which was the collateral and consequence of forsaking God. The law of God had been laid aside. Lawlessness resulted. Treating their fellow human beings inhumanely was a consequence of not walking in the fear and love of God. 'They sell the righteous for silver, and the needy for a pair of shoes. They that trample the head of the poor into the dust of the earth, and turn aside the way of the afflicted; a man and his father go into the same maiden, so that my holy name is profaned' (Amos 2:6b–7).

The prophets condemned nominal religion. Practising the externals of the faith was meaningless, they said, if the heart was not right—if they did not have a personal relationship with God. 'For I desire steadfast love and not sacrifice, the knowledge of God, rather than burnt offerings' (Hosea 6:6). And Micah 6:8 almost encapsulates the message of the prophets when it says: 'He has showed you, O man, what is good; and what does the Lord require of you but to do justice, and to love kindness, and to walk humbly with your God?'

The Messiah is coming!

The prophets foretold the coming of the promised Messiah. The promise of a Redeemer, which first occurred way back in Eden, continued to be made by God. The prophets took up the torch. The Messiah would come and put things right! Micah 5:2 stated that He would be born in Bethlehem. Isaiah 7:14 predicted that He would be born of a virgin. Jeremiah 31 foretold that in the future, God would establish a new covenant with His people. He would forgive their sins and even change their hearts so that they would obey and delight in Him from the heart. Then Isaiah 53 foretold that the coming Messiah—the Servant of the Lord—would redeem His people by bearing the consequences of their sin upon Himself. Forgiveness

By the waters of Babylon, there we sat down and wept, when we remembered Zion. On the willows there we hung up our lyres. For there our captors required of us songs, and our tormentors, mirth, saying, 'Sing us one of the songs of Zion!' How shall we sing the Lord's song in a foreign land? (Psalm 137:1–4).

The above Psalm relates something of the sorrow felt by some of God's people when they were exiled from the Promised Land. The exile refers to the time when thousands of the people of Israel were deported to Babylon. The Babylonians, under King Nebuchadnezzar, were now the dominant world power. In 597 BC, they conquered Israel and took her citizens captive to Babylon—'a foreign land'. Then, in 586 BC, the Babylonians destroyed Jerusalem and razed her glorious temple to the ground. The mourning, grief, shock and bereavement which this caused may be seen in its poetic articulation in the Lamentations of Jeremiah. 'The enemy has stretched out his hands over all her precious things; yea, she has seen the nations invade her sanctuary ...' (Lamentations 1:10). Behind it all however, and looking beyond all secondary causes, was the hand of God Himself:

The Lord has done what He purposed, has carried out His threat; as He ordained long ago, He has demolished without pity (Lamentations 2:17).

The reasons for the exile

The people of Israel were exiled because of their disobedience to their God and unfaithfulness to the covenant He had made with them.

During the time of Moses many years before, God had warned them:

> If you forget the Lord your God and go after other gods and serve them and worship them, I solemnly warn you this day that you shall surely perish (Deuteronomy 8:19).

The people of Israel were exiled because of their disobedience to their God and unfaithfulness to the covenant He had made with them.

> If you will not obey the voice of the Lord your God or be careful to do all His commandments and His statues which I command you this day ... (Deuteronomy 28:15)

> The Lord will bring you, and your king whom you set over you, to a nation that neither you nor your fathers have known; and there you shall serve other gods, of wood and stone (Deuteronomy 28:36).

The prophetic warning was now fulfilled. Israel was overtaken by the Babylonians. They found themselves a long way from home—out of the Promised Land and in

Babylon, surrounded by Babylonian idols which were anathema to the Law of Moses.

'Judah was taken into exile out of its land' (2 Kings 25:21). Why? Because of their rebellion against God. He had sent prophets to warn them, but they disregarded their warnings.

> The LORD, the God of their fathers, sent persistently to them by His messengers, because He had compassion on His people and on His dwelling place; but they kept mocking the messengers of God, despising His words and scoffing at His prophets, till the wrath of the LORD rose against His people, till there was no remedy (2 Chronicles 36:15–16).

Similarities today?

All this surely has its parallels in our day. God has His gospel preachers. They proclaim the message of deliverance from eternal judgment through faith in Christ. Like the Old Testament prophets, they too warn. They exhort, 'Believe in the Lord Jesus and you will be saved' (Acts 16:31). It is not unknown, however, for them to experience hostility, apathy or mockery in response to their message. As in ancient Israel though, so today, the principle stands: 'He who is often reproved, yet stiffens his neck, will suddenly be broken beyond healing' (Proverbs 29:1).

God cannot be hindered

The purposes of God, however, remained during the time of the exile. He had promised in Eden and through

Through Jeremiah the prophet, God gave a future promise and hope.

Abraham and through His prophets that He would send a Redeemer who was descended from the people of Israel, and nothing could thwart Him from fulfilling His purposes of grace and glory. The exile was therefore not forever.

The exile did not mean the end of the people of Israel. Through Jeremiah the prophet, God gave a future promise and hope:

> For thus says the LORD: When seventy years are completed for Babylon, I will visit you and I will fulfil to you my promise and bring you back to this place. ... I know the plans I have for you, says the LORD, plans for welfare and not for evil, to give you a future and a hope ... I will restore your fortunes and gather you from all the nations and all the places where I have driven you, says the LORD, and I will bring you back to the place from which I sent you into exile (Jeremiah 29:10, 11, 14).

Likewise, the prophet Ezekiel had his famous graveyard vision during this time. Yes, it was as though the people of Israel were dead. 'Our bones are dried up, and our hope is lost; we are clean cut off' (Ezekiel 37:11b). But the future was as bright as the promises of God!

> Thus says the Lord God: Behold, I will open your graves, and raise you from your graves, O my people; and I will bring you home into the land of Israel. And you shall know that I am the LORD (Ezekiel 37:12–13).

And sure enough, in the sovereignty of God, after seventy years of exile in Babylon, Israel was indeed restored to the land promised to the descendants of Abraham.

Daniel in exile

The book of Daniel is set during the exile in Babylon. Daniel reveals that it is possible to stay faithful to God even in a very ungodly environment, for God Himself stays faithful to us. Daniel's three companions refused to bow down to Babylonian idols, as commanded by King Nebuchadnezzar. At all costs they would not break the first commandment. They were cast into a fiery furnace for their faithfulness.

Daniel reveals that it is possible to stay faithful to God even in a very ungodly environment.

But God miraculously preserved them. Christ Himself stood by them in the fiery furnace. The king was astonished and exclaimed, 'I see four men loose, walking in the midst of the fire, and they are not hurt; and the appearance of the fourth is like a son of the gods' (Daniel 3:25). Nebuchadnezzar's faith in his Babylonian idols weakened and his heart was inclined towards the living God.

Later, and now under the rule of Darius the Mede, when Daniel had risen high up in society, he was thrown into a den of lions for his persistence in praying to the Lord God of Israel. But again, the Lord God performed a miracle of protection and preservation. It made an impression on Darius, and he confessed that it is the Lord God who is the true ruler of the universe:

For He is the living God, enduring for ever; His kingdom shall never be destroyed, and His dominion shall be to the end. He delivers and rescues, He works signs and wonders in heaven and on earth, He who saved Daniel from the power of the lion's (Daniel 6:26–27).

The exile

The exile refers to the seventy years God's people spent as captives in Babylon. It was a time of chastisement. It wrought repentance in some—history shows that Israel was never guilty of idolatry again. It was a time of longing to return home.

Interestingly, in the New Testament, Peter describes Christians in a way that echoes the people of God in Babylon. Christians, he says, are 'aliens and exiles' (1 Peter 2:11).

Aliens? Yes, for we do not belong to this fallen world and are considered as strangers by those who do.

Exiles? Yes, for we are far from home. For the Christian, heaven is our ultimate home.

Heaven is the dwelling place of God Himself. It is His nearer presence. And by the grace of God in Christ, heaven is a prepared place for a prepared people.

The Return
from Exile
540 BC

Chapter 13

When the Lord brought back those who returned
to Zion (margin) we were like those who dream.
Then our mouth was filled with laughter, and our
tongue with shouts of joy; then they said among
the nations, 'The Lord has done great things for
them.' The Lord has done great things for us; we
are glad (Psalm 126:1–3).

The above verses express something of the joy and
exuberance experienced by God's people when,
under the sovereignty of God, their exile in Babylon came
to an end and they returned to the Promised Land. God
had promised, 'When seventy years are completed for
Babylon, I will visit you, and I will fulfil to you my promise
and bring you back to this place' (Jeremiah 29:10). And
God kept his word. How? Through a change of world rulers.
Ultimately it is Almighty God who is in sovereign control
of this world, and He 'brings princes to nought, and makes
the rulers of the earth as nothing' (Isaiah 40:23).

In 539 BC, Cyrus, the king of Persia conquered Babylon.
The Persians were not in charge and the change of rule
brought about a change of policy. Nations exiled by the
Babylonians—including God's people—were allowed to
return home. It was the will of King Cyrus. Ultimately, it
was the will and working of God:

Now in the first year of Cyrus king of Persia, that
the word of the Lord by the mouth of Jeremiah
might be accomplished, the Lord stirred up the

spirit of Cyrus king of Persia so that he made a proclamation throughout all his kingdom and also put it in writing: 'Thus says Cyrus king of Persia, "The LORD, the God of heaven, has given me all the kingdoms of the earth, and He has charged me to build a house at Jerusalem, which is in Judah. Whoever is among you of all His people, may the LORD his God be with him. Let him go up"' (2 Chronicles 36:22–23).

And so began the return to Jerusalem and the Promised Land. Much building work—or rebuilding work—had to be done, as the Babylonians had razed Jerusalem and its temple to the ground. Under God however, and three key workers, the needed rebuilding work was accomplished. These three key workers were Zerubbabel, Ezra and Nehemiah.

Zerubbabel—rebuilding the temple

Under Zerubbabel, the foundations of the temple at Jerusalem were laid once again. Zerubbabel worked hand in hand with Jeshua the high priest.

Zerubbabel and Joshua, thus, put God first. Their first priority on returning to Jerusalem was to build 'the altar of the God of Israel to offer burnt offerings upon it, as it is written in the Law of Moses the man of God' (Ezra 3:2). Zerubbabel and Joshua, thus, put God first. They knew the necessity of

126

atonement for sin if fellowship with God is to be attained. They knew the importance of sacrifice in the divine economy—the sacrifice which could not be offered in Babylon. The rebuilding of the temple, however, was not all plain sailing. It was a case of 'fits and starts'. There was opposition from the non-Jews in the land, who accused the builders of sedition. To encourage the builders, God raised up two prophets at this time: Haggai and Zechariah.

Now the prophets, Haggai and Zechariah, the son of Iddo, prophesied to the Jews who were in Judea and Jerusalem in the name of the God of Israel who was over them. Then Zerubbabel the son of Shealtiel and Jeshua the son of Jozadak arose and began to rebuild the house of God which is in Jerusalem ... (Ezra 5:1–2).

Through these prophets, God encouraged the people and assured them of His presence:

Take courage, all you people of the land, says the LORD; work, for I am with you, says the LORD of hosts, according to the promise that I made you when you came out of Egypt. My Spirit abides among you; fear not (Haggai 2:4–5).

And Scripture then records:

The elders of the Jews built and prospered, through the prophesying of Haggai the prophet and Zechariah the son of Iddo. They finished their building by command of the God of Israel ... (Ezra 6:14)

... the returned exiles celebrated the dedication of this house of God with joy (Ezra 6:16).

And they kept the feast of unleavened bread seven days with joy; for the LORD had made them joyful (Ezra 6:22).

Ezra—rebuilding the people

Who was Ezra? He was a man of God who had a zeal for the Word of God and the glory of God and the spiritual welfare of His people. He too returned to the Promised Land. 'Ezra ... was a scribe skilled in the law of Moses which the LORD the God of Israel had given' (Ezra 7:6).

Scripture reveals Ezra as a great and zealous spiritual leader. His concern was not just with the peoples' return to the land, but that they should also return to the Word

His concern was not just with the peoples' return to the land, but that they should also return to the Word of God and the God of the Word.

of God and the God of the Word. 'For Ezra had set his heart to study the Law of the LORD, and to do it, and to teach His statues and ordinances in Israel' (Ezra 7:10). Here then was a man of diligence, obedience and influence. Ezra 9 and Nehemiah 9 reveal him as a great man of prayer, who grieved over both his own and the nations sins.

Nehemiah 8 records Ezra's public proclamation of the Word of God. He was some public speaker. They told Ezra the scribe to bring the book of the Law of Moses which the Lord had given to Israel (Nehemiah 8:1).

> Ezra the priest brought the law before the assembly, both men and women and all who could hear with understanding... (Nehemiah 8:2).

> And Ezra the scribe stood on a wooden pulpit (Nehemiah 8:4). And Ezra opened the book in the sight of all the people... (Nehemiah 8:5).

Thus, if Zerubbabel was a temple builder, and Nehemiah—as we shall see—was a wall builder, Ezra was a people builder. Scripture shows that, both in his prayers and his preaching, his main motivation was that the people return to the Lord their God. 'And day by day, from the first day to the last day, he read from the book of the law of God' (Nehemiah 8:18). This also led him to preach against the 'unequal yoke'—mixed marriages. Mixed marriages were forbidden by the law of Moses. When God's people marry those who do not belong to the living God, it is to their spiritual detriment. It may have been painful surgery, but the people acted on Ezra's word. 'When the people heard the law, they separated from Israel all those of foreign descent' (Nehemiah 13:3). The name Ezra means 'help'. Ezra lived up to his name and helped Israel return to the Lord and His ways.

> And the Israelites separated themselves from all foreigners, and stood and confessed their sins and the iniquities of their fathers (Nehemiah 9:2).

Nehemiah—rebuilding the walls

Nehemiah was a man of prayer and work and work and prayer. Scripture reveals him to be a man who had a great zeal for God's city of Jerusalem, and for the welfare

Nehemiah was a man of prayer and work and work and prayer.

of God's people. His return to Jerusalem was, 'to seek the welfare of the children of Israel' (Nehemiah 2:10), and he was motivated by an overriding zeal for the glory of God.

Nehemiah was in exile in Babylon, but Babylon had now come under Persian rule. He was obviously a trustworthy man, as he had been appointed cupbearer to King Artaxerxes. On hearing about the dilapidated state of Jerusalem in his homeland, however, Nehemiah was grief stricken, and turned to God in repentant prayer, pleading the covenant that God had made with Israel. His prayer to God was instrumental in gaining him favour with King Artaxerxes, who granted him permission to return to Jerusalem. It was all under the providence of God. Nehemiah testified, 'The king granted me what I asked, for the good hand of my God was upon me' (Nehemiah 2:8).

On returning to Jerusalem, and making a night-time inspection of the city, Nehemiah found that the report concerning Jerusalem was true. 'The walls of Jerusalem ... were broken down and its gates ... had been destroyed by fire' (Nehemiah 2:13). The city of God was dilapidated, unprotected and open to enemy attack. The book of Nehemiah relates how Nehemiah started out on his main life's work. Under Nehemiah's rallying and inspiring his people, the walls and gates of Jerusalem were rebuilt.

> Then I said to them 'You see the trouble we are in, how Jerusalem lies in ruins with its gates burned. Come, let us build the wall of Jerusalem, that we may no longer suffer disgrace' (Nehemiah 2:17).

Rebuilding Jerusalem was not easy. They faced enemies without and discouragement within. They needed to be on their guard. It was a case of both the sword and the trowel—building and defending. 'Those who carried burdens were laden in such a way that each with one hand laboured on the work and with the other held his weapon' (Nehemiah 4:17). Nehemiah comes over as God's man for the hour—a man of both prayer and action: a fearless leader and organiser.

The book of Nehemiah may be summarised using Nehemiah's own words: 'So we built the wall ... For the people had a mind to work' (Nehemiah 4:6). Nehemiah's prayers were answered, and God granted them success.

> The wall was finished on the twenty-fifth day of the month Elul, in fifty-two days. And when all our enemies heard of it, all the nations round about us were afraid and fell greatly in their own esteem; for they perceived that this work had been accomplished with the help of our God (Nehemiah 6:15–16).

The end of the beginning?

Old Testament history ends with the book of Nehemiah. Israel was back in the land, but God's promise of a Redeemer He had made in Eden; to Abraham to David; and foretold by the prophets, had not yet been fulfilled. The last book of the Old Testament is the prophecy of Malachi. It reveals again that apostasy and apathy had set in. Yet, it also contains the Messianic hope. God promised that 'the sun of righteousness shall rise, with healing in its wings' (Malachi 4:2). The godly still clung to God's promises. God would surely keep His Word. So, a remnant—like Simeon —waited patiently, 'looking for the consolation of Israel' (Luke 2:25); that is, they anticipated the coming of the Messiah!

So, a remnant— like Simeon —waited patiently; they anticipated the coming of the Messiah!

The Birth of the
Lord Jesus Christ
4 BC

Chapter 14

Promise and fulfilment

In Galatians 4:4–5 we read:

> But when the time had fully come, God sent forth His Son, born of woman, born under the law, to redeem those who were under the law, so that we might receive adoption as sons.

We come now to an epochal moment in world history and a major milestone in the divine drama of redemption: the birth of the Lord Jesus Christ.

The birth of Christ did not occur in a vacuum. As we have already intimated, the promise of a coming Redeemer runs throughout the Old Testament. The Old Testament is one Messianic longing. In Eden, God promised Eve that one of her descendants would come and crush Satan's head, undoing the ravages which sin has caused and healing the rift between creature and creator. God promised Abraham that through one of his descendants all the earth would be blessed. God promised King David that a Greater than he would eventually come and, 'He shall build a house for my name, and I will establish the throne of His kingdom for ever' (2 Samuel 7:13). This promise of a coming King, however, predated David by years. On his death bed, Jacob prophesied, 'The sceptre shall not depart from Judah, nor the ruler's staff from between His feet, until He comes to Whom it belongs; and to Him shall be the obedience of the peoples' (Genesis 49:10). In Christ, all these and other prophecies and promises were most wonderfully fulfilled. In Christ, the longed-for Messiah came. In Christ, God kept His promises.

> For all the promises of God find their Yes in Him. That is why we utter the Amen through Him, to the glory of God (2 Corinthians 1:20).

The whole of the Old Testament Scriptures are concerned with the anticipation of the coming Messiah, while the whole of the New Testament Scriptures are concerned with the actual arrival of the Messiah and its glorious saving consequences and implications for the believer. The main planks on which the Bible is constructed are Creation, the Fall and Redemption. It is human sin which makes human redemption such a necessity. The rift between creature and creator needs to be healed. The main message of the Bible is of a divine intervention to remedy this desperate, dire and damnable situation. The overarching message of the Bible is that of God's salvation of His people through His promised Redeemer. The gospel in a nutshell is famously summarised in John 3:16 when it states:

The rift between creature and creator needs to be healed.

> For God so loved the world that He gave His only Son that whoever believes in Him should not perish but have eternal life.

How did Christ enter our world?

Scripture reveals that Christ entered our world via the womb of a virgin—the virgin Mary, His earthly mother. His being of course preceded His birth. As the eternal Son of God and second person of the Trinity, He always existed. In a moment of time though, and in a landmark in God's plan of salvation, He took upon Himself our human flesh. He was conceived by the Holy Spirit in the womb of the virgin Mary and born in an animal shelter—surprisingly— in Bethlehem of Judea. The *Shorter Catechism*[1] puts it concisely and precisely:

> Q. Who is the Redeemer of God's elect?
>
> A. The only Redeemer of God's elect is the Lord Jesus Christ, who, being the eternal Son of God, became man, and so was, and continueth to be, God and man in two distinct natures, and one person for ever.
>
> Q. How did Christ, being the Son of God, become man?
>
> A. Christ, the Son of God, became man, by taking to Himself a true body and a reasonable soul, being conceived by the power of the Holy Ghost, in the womb of the virgin Mary, and born of her, yet without sin'.

The virgin birth of Christ

Christ therefore was conceived in a supernatural manner. Isaiah had prophesied, 'Behold, a virgin shall conceive and bear a son, and shall call His name Immanuel' (Isaiah 7:14 KJV). When the time had fully come, the prophecy was fulfilled, when Christ was conceived by the Holy Spirit in the womb of the virgin Mary.

Mary—she was a young women based in Nazareth, who was engaged to be married to Joseph. The angel Gabriel explained to her: 'The Holy Spirit will come upon you, and the power of the Most High will overshadow you; therefore the child to be born will be called holy, the Son of God' (Luke 1:35).

Humanly speaking, virgin births are impossible. But here we are dealing with God, and 'with God nothing will be impossible' (Luke 1:37). The 'virgin birth' of Christ was an absolute necessity. Had He been conceived through the instrumentality of a human father, He would have inherited our human sin, for all the descendants of Adam inherit his fallen nature. Had Christ had a fallen nature, He would not have been able to be the Redeemer of sinners—His sacrifice of Himself would have been for His own sins, and not for the sins of others. The virgin conception of Christ therefore is a necessity and is totally in-line with His sinless life and atoning death. Scripture reveals Him as being 'holy, blameless, unstained, separated from sinners' (Hebrews 7:26) and 'like that of a lamb without blemish or spot'

> **The 'virgin birth' of Christ was an absolute necessity.**

(1 Peter 1:19). Scripture reveals that Christ alone, of all the children of men, was sinless. He alone was impeccable. He alone is qualified to be the Saviour of sinners.

Where did Christ enter our world?

Christ entered our world when He was born in the 'little town of Bethlehem', some seven miles southwest of Jerusalem. Again, this was just as a prophet of God had predicted. Seven hundred years BC, Micah the prophet was enabled by God to prophesy, 'But you, O Bethlehem Ephrathah, who are little to be among the clans of Judah, from you shall come forth for me One who is to be ruler in Israel, whose origin is from of old, from ancient days [lit. from everlasting] (Micah 5:2). The prophecy was fulfilled, 'when Jesus was born in Bethlehem of Judea in the days of Herod the king' (Matthew 2:1). Truly, prophecy is history written in advance. King David hailed from Bethlehem. For all his faults, David was considered Israel's greatest king. David, though, was just a foreshadow of Jesus, 'Great David's Greater Son'.[2] The angel Gabriel explained to Mary of Him that, 'The Lord God will give to Him the throne of His father David, and He will reign over the house of Jacob for ever, and of His kingdom there will be no end' (Luke 1:32–33). Christ is the ultimate ruler and authority. It is through Him that we enter God's glorious Kingdom. His Kingship is a facet of His being the longed-for Messiah.

Christ executeth the office of a king in subduing

us to Himself, in ruling and defending us, and in restraining and conquering all His and our enemies (*Shorter Catechism*[3]).

Lawson[4] comments:

A king is a ruler of a kingdom. Now there is a great kingdom set up on earth, consisting of all God's people, and its ruler is Christ. As such, His duties are here said to be threefold. 1. He makes us willing to obey Him. 2. He gives us laws for our guidance and safety. 3. He limits and finally puts down all who oppose us and Him.

Jesus shall reign where'ere the sun
Doth its successive journeys run
His kingdom stretch from shore to shore
Till moons shall wax and wane no more
(Isaac Watts 1674–1748).

Why did Christ enter our world?

The Bible leaves us in no doubt regarding the answer to the above question. 'Christ Jesus came into the world to save sinners' (1 Timothy 1:15). Jesus Himself said, 'The Son of man came to seek and to save the lost' (Luke 19:10). The clue is in Jesus' very name. The name Jesus means 'Saviour'. 'You shall call His name Jesus for He will save His people from their sins' (Matthew 1:21).

So, the Lord Jesus came into the world—He left heaven for earth—with a specific mission in mind. He came to accomplish the salvation of God's people. He came to save us from the condemnation we deserve because of our sins. He came to reconcile sinners to God. And how did He achieve this? Not by His birth at Bethlehem, but by His death at Calvary. In the Bible, all roads lead to Calvary, for salvation was achieved not by Christ's cradle but by His cross.

Salvation was achieved not by Christ's cradle but by His cross.

He was born to die—to pay the wages of His peoples' sins. And so, in our next chapter we turn to the death of Christ at Calvary.

The Death
of Christ
AD 30

Chapter 15

The centrality of the cross

In the Bible, all of the roads lead to the cross of Calvary. The central message of the Bible is that of God's gracious salvation of His people through the sending of the Messiah, the Lord Jesus Christ. And that salvation was achieved by the death of Christ at Calvary for all who believe.

Why were the holy Scriptures bequeathed to us at all? The Bible's own answer is because 'the sacred writings ... are able to instruct you for salvation through faith in Christ Jesus' (2 Timothy 3:15). And that salvation was procured not by Christ's life but by His death; not by His living, teaching or example, but by His atoning sacrifice. 'He has appeared once for all at the end of the age to put away sin by the sacrifice of Himself' (Hebrews 9:26).

The Bible: the Book of the cross

The death of Christ on the Cross—that is, His redeeming work—is integral to the Bible. It is part of its very warp and woof. It is more than a facet of the gospel. It is the gospel. It is prophesied and typified in the Old Testament; it is described in the Gospels; it is proclaimed in the Acts; it is explained and applied in the Epistles; and it is celebrated in the book of Revelation.

If we wanted to summarise the message of the Old Testament in one verse, we could do so by employing

Genesis 22:7: 'Where is the Lamb ...?', or perhaps the next verse: 'God will provide Himself the Lamb' (Genesis 22:8).

Then if we wanted to summarise the message of the New Testament in one verse, we could employ John 1:29: 'Behold, the Lamb of God who takes away the sin of the world', for the verses of the New Testament are given to point us to the sacrifice of Christ at Calvary.

And if we wanted to summarise the Christian's response of praise to the gracious salvation of God in Christ at Calvary, we could employ Revelation 5:12: 'Worthy is the Lamb who was slain, to receive power and wealth and wisdom and might and honour and glory and blessing!'

> My faith looks up to Thee
> Thou Lamb of Calvary
> Saviour divine!
> Now hear me while I pray
> Take all my guilt away
> O let me from this day
> Be wholly Thine
> (Ray Palmer 1808–1887)

The Lord Jesus lived under the shadow of the cross throughout His earthly life and ministry. His purpose in living was His dying.

His purpose in living was His dying.

His reason for coming to earth was the very last few hours of His earthly life, when He suffered and bled and died on a wooden cross. The cross of Christ, therefore, was no accident but an appointment. It had been foreordained by God. It was central to His plan of salvation to redeem a people for Himself. The Lord Jesus knew this, hence:

> Taking the twelve again, He began to tell them what was to happen to Him, saying, 'Behold, we are going up to Jerusalem; and the Son of man will be delivered to the chief priests and the scribes, and they will condemn Him to death, and deliver Him to the Gentiles; and they will mock Him and spit upon Him, and scourge Him and kill Him; and after three days He will rise' (Mark 10:32–34).

The Saviour's prediction was fulfilled to the absolute letter, down to the exact details.

The Gospel writers are sparing when it comes to describing the physical sufferings of Christ on the cross. The emphasis of the Bible is not so much Christ's physical sufferings—great though they were—but the spiritual suffering He underwent to redeem His people:

'He Himself bore our sins in His body on the tree' (1 Peter 2:24).

He was 'offered once to bear the sins of many' (Hebrews 9:28).

This means that He was made liable for His peoples' sins to save them from the dreadful liability that His people owed to God for their sins.

> There was no other good enough
> To pay the price of sin

145

> He only could unlock the gate
> Of heaven and let us in.
> (Mrs C F Alexander 1818–95).

Darkness and damnation

The Gospel writers record that when Christ died on the cross of Calvary:

> From the sixth hour there was darkness over all the land until the ninth hour. And about the ninth hour Jesus cried with a loud voice, 'Eli, Eli, lama sabachthani?' that is, 'My God, my God, why hast Thou forsaken Me' (Matthew 27:45–46).

This darkness at midday on a spring day can only be explained supernaturally. Darkness, in the Bible, refers to the judgment of God. The prophet Joel warned of the coming judgment of God for the unrepentant in these words: 'The day of the LORD is coming, it is near, a day of darkness and gloom, a day of clouds and thick darkness!' (Joel 2:1–2). Hell—the ultimate in God's judgement—is described in the Bible as, 'the outer darkness; there men will weep and gnash their teeth' (Matthew 8:12). That is, a darkness away from the light, love and life of God.

So, when Jesus died at Calvary, He experienced a terrible darkness. Why? To save others from the outer darkness. He was being judged by God for the sins of others, so that others might be saved from the judgement of God. He was separated from God to reconcile us to God. He was forsaken by God for us to procure the forgiveness of God for us. He suffered the curse of God on sin to redeem others from the curse of God on sin. 'Christ redeemed us from the curse of the law, having become a curse for us, for it is written, "Cursed be every one who hangs on a tree"' (Galatians 3:13).

He suffered the curse of God on sin to redeem others from the curse of God on sin.

God's justice demands that sin be punished, either in the sinner or in a substitute for the sinner. Christ thus died in the place of sinners. He died as the sinner's substitute. 'Christ died for our sins' (1 Corinthians 15:3). 'He was wounded for our transgressions' (Isaiah 53:5)—'to satisfy divine justice and reconcile us to God' (*Shorter Catechism*[1]).

When Christ endured the darkness of Calvary, He was actually enduring the wrath of God against sin to save the believer from the wrath of God against sin. It is 'Jesus who delivers us from the wrath to come' (1 Thessalonians 1:10). 'For God has not destined us for wrath, but to obtain salvation through our Lord Jesus Christ' (1 Thessalonians 5:9).

The cross of Christ alone turns aside the wrath of God that we deserve. The word which the New Testament uses to encapsulate this is the word *hilasmos*, which means 'propitiation'. To propitiate means to appease or satisfy— to turn the wrath and displeasure aside. The cross of

147

Christ, therefore, is the supreme demonstration of both the wrath of God and the love of God: the wrath of God in punishing sin; the love of God in providing a substitute for the sinner so that he might be pardoned.

> God shows His love for us in that while we were yet sinners Christ died for us (Romans 5:8).

In this is love, not that we loved God but that He loved us and sent His Son to be the propitiation for our sins (1 John 4:10 KJV).

The death of Christ at Calvary. It is both a historical and a historic event. The cross of Christ refers to the redeeming work of Christ—what He underwent to achieve the eternal salvation of all who trust in Him. It is the central theme of the whole Bible. It is the heart of the Christian gospel which the church is commissioned and committed to proclaim—'we preach Christ crucified' (1 Corinthians 1:23). It is and forever will be the glory of all who have come to know its saving power. But far be it from me to glory except in the cross of our Lord Jesus Christ, by which the world has been crucified to me and I to the world (Galatians 6:14).

The cross of Christ ... is the heart of the Christian gospel which the church is commissioned and committed to proclaim.

> Death and the curse were in our cup
> O Christ 'twas full for Thee!

But Thou hast drained the last dark drop
'Tis empty now for me
That bitter cup, love drank it up
Now blessing's draught for me.

The tempest's awful voice was heard
O Christ, it broke on Thee!
Thy open bosom was my ward
It braved the storm for me
Thy form was scarred, Thy visage marred
Now cloudless peace for me.

Jehovah bade His sword awake
O Christ, it woke 'gainst Thee!
Thy blood the flaming blade must slake
Thy heart its sheath must be
All for my sake my peace to make
Now sleeps that sword for me.

The Holy One did hide His face
O Christ 'twas hid from Thee!
Dumb darkness wrapt Thy soul a space
The darkness due to me
But now that face of radiant grace
Shines forth in light on me.
(Anne Ross Cousin 1824–1906).

The Resurrection
of Christ
AD 30

The Christian faith of the Bible is founded and grounded on the resurrection of Christ from the dead. If the Christ, who died at Calvary and was subsequently buried in the tomb of Joseph of Arimathea, had remained dead in that tomb, the New Testament would have never been written at all, and the redemption promises of God, made in the Old Testament, would not have been fulfilled. If the Christ who died at Calvary became just a decomposing and decomposed corpse, the Christian faith is a failed faith, and Christ's death was not actually an eternally atoning sacrifice for sins. As the Apostle put it:

> If Christ has not been raised, your faith is futile and you are still in your sins. Then those also who have fallen asleep in Christ have perished. If for this life only we have hoped in Christ, we are of all men most to be pitied (1 Corinthians 15:17–19).

But Paul then goes on to affirm:

> But in fact Christ has been raised from the dead ... (1 Corinthians 15:20).

He is the living and eternal life-giving Saviour. Paul knew this as he had had a dramatic encounter with the glorified, transformed and transforming Christ on the Damascus Road—as we shall see in a subsequent chapter.

Cause and effect

Every effect has a cause. How do we account for the existence of the New Testament Scriptures? How do we account for the transformation which came over Jesus' disciples? After the crucifixion of Jesus, they were downcast, dejected and defeated. They locked themselves away in their grief, disappointment and fear. Later, though, we see them boldly proclaiming the same Jesus as being mighty to save. The majority of them were eventually martyred for so doing. Did they really willingly give their lives for a Christ who they proclaimed to be alive, when they secretly knew He was dead? Hardly! Then how do we account for the growth of the Christ church both in the New Testament and in subsequent world history up until the present day? How, also, do we account for the change of the Sabbath Day from the seventh day of the week to the first day of the week—the day on which Christ arose? Who would dare tamper with a commandment of God? Only one cause explains all these and other effects: the resurrection of the Lord Jesus Christ,

> ... that Christ died for our sins in accordance with the Scriptures, that He was buried, that He was raised on the third day in accordance with the Scriptures (1 Corinthians 15:3, 4).

The Christ who was crucified on the first Good Friday,

Did they really willingly give their lives for a Christ who they proclaimed to be alive, when they secretly knew He was dead?

and whose dead body was laid in a tomb, most certainly conquered the grave on the following Easter Sunday.

Evidence for the resurrection

The resurrection of Christ is a major milestone in the grand drama of divine redemption and also an epochal landmark in world history. It was an event of the most momentous consequences. The evidence for the resurrection of Christ is manifold but may be broadly summarised under two main categories:

1. Christ's tomb was found to be empty.
2. The risen Christ was seen, heard and touched, and He even ate.

Hence, the resurrection of Christ was a real, bodily resurrection. He really lived and lives—He does not just 'live on' as a memory or an influence.

It is remarkable that the first people who witnessed both the empty tomb of Christ and met up with the risen Saviour Himself were ... women. 'Toward the dawn of the first day of the week, Mary Magdalene and the other Mary went to see the sepulchre' (Matthew 28:1). Their intention was to anoint the dead body of Jesus. In spite of Christ's predictions, the last thing they expected was that He would rise from the dead and that they would encounter Him. Astonishingly though, an angel from heaven met them at the tomb. He had rolled away the great stone that had secured the Saviour's grave. Matthew then records:

153

> The angel said to the women, 'Do not be afraid; for
> I know that you seek Jesus who was crucified. He is
> not here; for He has risen, as He said. Come, see the
> place where He lay' (Matthew 28:5–6).

When they ran away excitedly to tell the disciples,
Matthew next records:

> And behold, Jesus met them and said, 'Hail!'
> And they came up and took hold of His feet and
> worshipped Him (Matthew 28:9).

The first witnesses of the empty tomb and risen, living
Christ then, were women. Considering the low status
which women had in the patriarchal society of Bible
times, this has all the hallmarks of authenticity. No one
would have invented this. Here is God's truth not man's
tale. Here is fact not fiction. Here is the greatest and most
monumental fact of history—His story.

Scripture goes on to record the risen Saviour's
subsequent appearances to His fearful and disheartened
remaining disciples, who were locked away in the Upper
Room. Scripture also records the risen Christ's appearance
to two downcast disciples on the Emmaus Road. And
Scripture also records how the risen Christ entertained
Peter—the one who had failed his Master abysmally—eating
a breakfast meal with him on the shore of the Sea of Galilee.
Scripture even states that, 'He appeared to more than five
hundred brethren at one time, most of whom are still alive'
(1 Corinthians 15:6). Paul is referring to five hundred who

hallucinated all together at the same time? Hardly. No! The resurrection of Christ has rightly been called 'the most attested fact of history'. It cannot be explained away. 'He presented Himself alive after His passion by many proofs' (Acts 1:3). The resurrection of Christ just cannot be refuted, no matter how hard sceptics try and no matter how hard determined unbelief attempts to do so:

> Hallelujah! Hallelujah!
> Hearts to heaven and voices raise
> Sing to God a hymn of gladness
> Sing to God a hymn of praise
> He who on the cross a victim
> For the world's salvation bled
> Jesus Christ, the King of glory
> Now is risen from the dead.
> (Christopher Wordsworth 1807–85).

The most momentous event

The resurrection of Christ is both the most attested fact of history and the most momentous fact of history. Its implications are wide-ranging and far reaching. In what way is this so? Let us consider:

THE DEITY OF CHRIST

Christ's conquest of the grave is the ultimate proof of His deity—

The resurrection of Christ is both the most attested fact of history and the most momentous fact of history.

155

that He was and is none other than the very Son of God. He claimed to be God by both explicit statements and by implication. His claims were vindicated. He was the 'designated Son of God in power according to the Spirit of holiness by His resurrection from the dead' (Romans 1:4). He once asserted, 'I am the resurrection and the life; he who believes in me, though he die, yet shall he live, and whoever lives and believes in me shall never die' (John 11:25–26). His bodily resurrection confirms that His claim was no idle claim.

THE WORTH OF HIS WORK

The resurrection of Christ reveals the pleasure and acceptance of God the Father with His Son's atoning death. The resurrection is the divine endorsement of Christ's finished work of redemption. Payment for sin was fully made. Atonement for sin was completely secured. He 'was put to death for our trespasses and raised for our justification' (Romans 4:25). Had Christ remained in the grave, His death would have been as a martyr for a cause and not an atonement for sin. But Jesus rose, so our sins are forgiven:

Had Christ remained in the grave, His death would have been as a martyr for a cause and not an atonement for sin.

> Our Surety freed declares us free

For whose offences He was seized
In His release our own we see
And shout to view jehovah pleased.
(Johan Olaf Wallin 1779–1839).

THE BELIEVER'S FUTURE RESURRECTION

Christ's resurrection is the pledge and pattern of the guaranteed future resurrection of all who belong to Him. Our bodies at the moment are subject to illness, pain and ultimately death. But they will not always be so!

> Christ has been raised from the dead, the first fruits of those who have fallen asleep (1 Corinthians 15:20).

We will thus follow Christ. His resurrection body was, paradoxically the same but different. He was recognised as Jesus, yet His resurrection body was not subject to the normal human limitations. Neither will ours be, if we belong to Jesus, for when He comes again, He '... will change our lowly body to be like His glorious body, by the power which enables Him even to subject all things to Himself' (Philippians 3:21).

At the resurrection, believers, being raised up in glory, shall be openly acknowledged and acquitted in the day of judgement, and made perfectly blessed in the full enjoying of God for all eternity (*Shorter Catechism*[1]).

For the Christian, the best is yet to be. The Christian's thrilling prospect is being raised to new life and immortality: redeemed bodies on a redeemed earth. Christ's resurrection is the pledge—the first fruits—of better things to come.

At the heart of the Christian faith lies both the cross of Christ and the empty tomb of Christ.

So, at the heart of the Christian faith lies both the cross of Christ and the empty tomb of Christ. When we think of the one, we should think of the other. They are the two sides of the one salvation coin. They both tell us of a salvation fully accomplished. They both remind us of the uniqueness—the incomparability of the faith of the Bible. They are also the fuel for Christian praise, both here and hereafter:

Christ is risen, Christ the first fruits
Of the holy harvest field
Which will all its full abundance
At His second coming yield

Then the golden ears of harvest
Will their heads before Him wave
Ripened by His glorious sunshine
From the furrows of the grave

Hallelujah! Hallelujah!
Glory be to God on high
Hallelujah to the Saviour
Who has gained the victory

Hallelujah to the Spirit
Fount of love and sanctity
Hallelujah! Hallelujah!
To the Triune Majesty!
(Christopher Wordsworth 1774–1846)

The Coming of
the Holy Spirit

After the death, resurrection and ascension of the Lord Jesus back to heaven—interestingly, Scripture reveals that He both entered into and exited from the earth in a supernatural manner—the next milestone in the biblical story is the pouring out of God's Holy Spirit on the earth. The Holy Spirit had been active in achieving God's purposes ever since creation, when 'the Spirit of God was moving over the face of the waters' (Genesis 1:2), but the gospel age, which began at Pentecost, is specifically the age of the Holy Spirit. The salvation which Christ procured was now to be a salvation proclaimed. But it was to be proclaimed in the power of the Holy Spirit. Jesus' last words and marching orders to His disciples was the commandment to, 'Go into all the world and preach the gospel ...' (Mark 16:15). They were to proclaim the salvation He procured and exhort sinners to avail themselves of it. Yet they were not to do this straight away. Yes, 'repentance and forgiveness of sins should be preached in His name to all nations' (Luke 24:47), but Jesus also said that they should 'stay in the city, until you are clothed with power from on high' (Luke 24:49). He was referring to the mighty assistance they would need and the mighty assistance they would receive and the mighty assistance which the Holy Spirit alone could give, as they went about their gospel endeavours for Christ. Similarly, just before His ascension, Jesus also promised:

But you shall receive power when the Holy Spirit

has come upon you, and you shall be my witnesses in Jerusalem and in all Judea and Samaria and to the end of the earth (Acts 1:8).

Pentecost

Jesus' promise was fulfilled. On the day of Pentecost—fifty days after His resurrection—the Holy Spirit came in power. The remaining disciples were indeed empowered. Subsequently, the book of Acts reveals how the gospel of Christ spread abroad, and sinners were saved and churches established through the apostles' exploits. The gospel reached Rome, the centre of the then known world. And from there, Roman soldiers, who had been converted, took the good news of Christ to the edges of the empire—'to the end of the earth'.

Pentecost, therefore—when the Holy Spirit of God was poured out on the earth—is another major milestone in the divine saga of redemption. Acts chapter two relates this epochal event. The disciples of Jesus, and a few others,

... were all together in one place. And suddenly a sound came from heaven like the rush of a mighty wind, and it filled all the house where they were sitting. And there appeared to them tongues as of fire, distributed and resting on each one of them. And they were all filled with the Holy Spirit and began to speak in other tongues, as the Spirit gave them utterance (Acts 2:1–4).

Our tongue is essential for our speech and communication. The Holy Spirit's coming in 'tongues as of fire' shows that His purpose is that of communication. It is He who communicates the message of the gospel to human hearts and minds. It is He who makes Jesus real to us, showing us our need of Christ and the Christ for our need. The God of the Bible is a communicating God. God communicates via His Holy Spirit, through the word of the gospel. The Holy Spirit, however, does not draw attention to Himself. He draws attention to Christ. Jesus said of Him:

> *It is He [the Holy Spirit] who makes Jesus real to us, showing us our need of Christ and the Christ for our need.*

> When the Spirit of truth comes, He will guide you into all the truth; ... He will glorify Me, for He will take what is mine and declare it to you (John 16:13, 14).

Notice that the Holy Spirit came in 'tongues as of fire'. Here we glimpse the deity of the Holy Spirit. He is a divine Person—the third Person of the Trinity. God's presence in the wilderness with Israel in Old Testament times was by means of a cloud in the daytime and a 'pillar of fire by night' (Exodus 13:22). Fire, of course, is formidable. It is not to be trifled with. Scripture says, 'Our God is a consuming fire' (Hebrews 12:29). Fire also takes away the impurities from metal—it refines. Salvation entails

163

having our sins and impurities taken away, making us fit for fellowship with a holy God.

Luke also records that at Pentecost the Holy Spirit came as 'a mighty wind' (Acts 2:2). A mighty wind can be very destructive. But a mighty wind can also be constructive. It can drive a turbine and produce electricity. The Holy Spirit's power is a constructive, creative one. 'You shall receive power when the Holy Spirit has come upon you, and you shall be my witnesses ...' (Acts 1:8), said Jesus. And His words were fulfilled. The Holy Spirit came and transformed the disciples into dynamic witnesses of Christ and fearless proclaimers of the gospel, instrumental in the salvation of others. Consider. The Bible records Peter's cowardly denial of Christ before a maid. Courage failed him. He was no witness for Christ. But, after Pentecost, Peter was transformed. On the day of Pentecost, he boldly proclaimed Christ, and three thousand souls were saved. In Acts 4, we likewise see him fearlessly proclaiming the crucified, risen Christ before the Jewish religious authorities. He told them straight, 'There is salvation in no one else, for there is no other name under heaven given among men by which we must be saved' (Acts 4:12). Luke notes that the Jewish rulers 'saw the boldness of Peter and John' (Acts 4:13). What is the explanation for such a transformation in Peter? Luke gives us the clue when he

The Holy Spirit's power is a constructive, creative one.

prefaces Peter's speech with, 'Then Peter, filled with the Holy Spirit, said to them "Rulers of the people and elders ..."' (Acts 4:8). He had received the empowering of the Holy Spirit of God, just as Jesus promised.

The Acts of the Holy Spirit

The following chapters of Acts go on to record the continuing activity of the Holy Spirit in saving souls and establishing churches. He was the One who empowered and enabled the apostles to be instruments in doing this. The full title of Acts is really 'The Acts of the Risen Christ, through His Apostles, by the Holy Spirit.'

The Holy Spirit of God, therefore, was God's agent of salvation at the time of the early church, just as He is today. His work in the scheme of salvation is indispensable. While Christ has procured salvation, it is the Holy Spirit who puts us into actual, personal possession of that salvation. 'We are made partakers of the redemption purchased by Christ, by the effectual application of it to us by His Holy Spirit' (*Shorter Catechism*[1]).

The indispensable Spirit

The apostles worked. They preached the gospel in ever expanding fields. But their labours would have been in vain unless the Holy Spirit had ministered through their endeavours. No human being can save a soul. Jesus said, 'It is the Spirit that gives life, the flesh is of no avail' (John

6:63). The Spirit of God alone can convict us of our sin and need of Christ, and nurture in us saving faith in the Christ who is the answer to our need.

A little later on, after Paul had preached in Thessalonica, he reminded the Christians there how 'our gospel came to you not only in word, but also in power and in the Holy Spirit and with full conviction' (1 Thessalonians 1:5). For preaching to be effectual two things are necessary:

Faithfulness to the gospel on the preacher's part. The Holy Spirit's influence and accompaniment on God's part.

The preacher's efforts may fall on deaf ears, and the hearers may respond with either hostility or apathy. But not when God's Holy Spirit is at work. His call is always effectual. We may distinguish between the outward call of the preacher, and the inward call of the Holy Spirit. The former is often ineffectual, the latter never so. To quote the *Shorter Catechism* again:

> Effectual calling is the work of God's Spirit whereby, convincing us of our sin and misery, enlightening our minds in the knowledge of Christ and renewing our wills, He doth persuade and enable us to embrace Jesus Christ, freely offered to us in the Gospel[2].

The Spirit of God maketh the reading, but especially the preaching of the Word an effectual means of convincing and converting sinners, and of building them up in holiness and comfort, through faith, unto salvation[3].

So, the promised Holy Spirit came in power at Pentecost. He ushered in the gospel age—the age of the Spirit. He empowered and enabled and emboldened the early Christians to preach the gospel and bear witness to Christ. And the church of Christ was built. 'The Lord added to their number day by day those who were being saved' (Acts 2:47). Christian salvation is a matter of a divine redemption: divinely accomplished and divinely applied. It was accomplished by Christ at Calvary. It is applied to human souls by the Holy Spirit of God. The Bible reveals that the Holy Spirit is indispensable in relation to both Christian salvation and Christian service.

He empowered and enabled and emboldened the early Christians to preach the gospel and bear witness to Christ.

> To God the Spirit's Name
> Immortal worship give
> Whose new-creating power
> Makes the dead sinner live
> His work completes the great design
> And fills the soul with joy divine.
> (Isaac Watts 1674–1748).

Paul

After the death and resurrection of Christ, one of the most significant and far-reaching events in world history—and certainly in the biblical story, and divine drama of redemption—is the conversion of Saul of Tarsus to the Christian faith. This was to prove to be an event of immeasurable consequences. Only eternity will reveal the debt that we owe—under God—to Paul, as Saul was also known. His conversion changed him from being a great opponent of the Christian faith to being the greatest exponent of the Christian faith. Thirteen of his letters, to churches and individuals, are contained in the New Testament. In these, he explains, applies, defends and proclaims the salvation of Christ, which he had come to know and enjoy. Christ was the absolute centre of Paul's life. He could say, 'For to me to live is Christ, and to die is gain' (Philippians 1:21). Paul's driving motivation was 'that I may know Him ...' (Philippians 3:10) and make Him better known. His engine was the will of God. He could even say, 'I do not account my life of any value nor as precious to myself, if only I may accomplish my course and the ministry which I received from the Lord Jesus, to testify to the gospel of the grace of God' (Acts 20:24). Paul's Christian life, however, had a distinct starting point; he had a dramatic encounter with the risen, glorified Christ on the Damascus Road.

Paul the persecutor

It is understating it to say that Paul was not always a

Christian. At one time he was vehemently opposed to both Christians and the Christian faith. He was a strict Jew by birth, nurture and conviction. He was a Pharisee, or 'separated one', zealous for the Lord God of Israel. His strict monotheism, he believed, was incompatible with worshipping the Lord Jesus as God. Christians were blasphemers! They should be rooted out. Thus, when Stephen, the first Christian martyr, was stoned to death, 'Saul was consenting to his death' (Acts 8:1). Acts 9:1 then records Saul's 'breathing threats and murder against the disciples of the Lord'. In his own words, Paul confessed that he once 'persecuted the church of God violently and tried to destroy it' (Galatians 1:13). And later again, while under arrest, he reported that same thing—that he 'persecuted this Way to the death ... and journeyed to Damascus to take those also who were there and bring them in bonds to Jerusalem to be punished' (Acts 22:4, 5). But it was while he was journeying to Damascus to persecute Christians that Paul had his dramatic, life- and world-changing encounter with the Christ whom the Christians worshipped. Luke reports this in Acts 9, and Paul related this himself those few years later when he gave a public testimony to what had happened to him:

> As I made my journey near to Damascus, about noon a great light from heaven suddenly shone about me. And I fell to the ground and heard a voice saying to me, 'Saul, Saul, why do you persecute

me?' And I answered, 'Who are you, Lord?' And He said to me, 'I am Jesus of Nazareth whom you are persecuting' (Acts 22:6–8).

So, the glorified Christ appeared to Paul. He realised how wrong he had been and his life took an about-turn. The persecutor of Christians soon became a preacher of Christ. He travelled to Damascus with a view to destroying the church. But now he made friends with the Christians there. They were his brothers and sisters.

> *The persecutor of Christians soon became a preacher of Christ.*

For several days he was with the disciples at Damascus (Acts 9:19).

And in the synagogues immediately he proclaimed Jesus, saying 'He is the Son of God' (Acts 9:20). ... and confounded the Jews who lived in Damascus by proving that Jesus was the Christ (Acts 9:22).

Paul therefore had a new confession. Christians were not blasphemers. His encounter with Christ left him in no doubt that He was indeed the Son of God and God the Son. And his encounter with Christ also enlightened him to the fact that Jesus exactly fitted the promises of the Messiah, foretold in the Scriptures Paul knew so well. Jesus was indeed the Messiah—the anointed prophet, priest and king, the Redeemer promised by God. It was life changing and it was in the plan of God. Paul was to be instrumental in bringing others to know the Christ he had encountered, and instrumental in building up the church of the Lord Jesus Christ. On the Damascus Road, Christ not only saved him, but also commissioned him. 'I have appeared to you for this purpose, to appoint you to serve and bear witness ...' (Acts 26:16). Specifically, Paul was called to go to the Gentiles—non-Jews—to tell them about the Saviour. Paul's upbringing in Tarsus, with its mix of culture, meant he could mix with them as easily as his fellow Jews. Under God he now had a task. It was:

> ... to open their eyes, that they may turn from darkness to light and from the power of Satan to God, that they may receive forgiveness of sins and a place among those who are sanctified by faith in Me (Acts 26:18).

Paul the pioneer

Paul's self-designation is that of 'an apostle of Christ Jesus by the will of God' (Ephesians 1:1 et al.). He also describes himself as 'a servant of Jesus Christ' (Romans 1:1). An apostle refers to 'a sent one' or an 'envoy'—one sent with a commission. The word 'servant' here is the word doulos or 'bond-slave'. Slavery was commonplace in New Testament times. Paul was saying that he was captive to the will of Jesus Christ his Master.

Over half of the book of Acts is given over to the

three missionary journeys that the Apostle Paul made. Interestingly, in Acts 16 we see him taking the gospel into what we now know as Europe. During these missionary journeys, we see him preaching the gospel, contending for the faith, gathering converts for Christ and nurturing these converts in their new-found faith—not to mention having to deal with much opposition, persecution and other difficulties.

Paul's missionary base was Antioch in Syria. Here, what today we would call his sending church was located. The church at Antioch was a multi-national one. Luke records that Paul was active in service here before he undertook his missionary travels. 'For a whole year they [Paul and Barnabas] met with the church, and taught a large company of people' (Acts 11:26). Then, very interestingly, Luke records: '... and in Antioch the disciples were for the first time called Christians' (Acts 11:26). The term Christian means 'Christ's one'. It may originally have been a nickname. A Christian, though, certainly is 'Christ's one', for a Christian is united to Christ by saving faith. Paul opens his letter to the church at Colossi, for instance, by saying, 'To the saints and faithful brethren in Christ at Colossae' (Colossians 1:2).

The term Christian means 'Christ's one'.

The Apostle Paul therefore was part of a church community. While being a pioneer and rugged individual, he was not individualistic or an isolated believer. His call and commission to be a missionary—an envoy and ambassador for Christ—came in a congregational setting, during a gathering of the church in Antioch. Luke states: 'While they were worshipping the Lord and fasting, the Holy Spirit said, "Set apart for me Barnabas and Saul for the work to which I have called them." Then after fasting and praying they laid their hands on them and sent them off' (Acts 13:2–3). Paul knew the prayerful, and no doubt practical, support and backing of a 'home church', to which he would return at the end of his missionary journeys. Acts records how:

> ... they sailed [back] to Antioch, where they had been commended to the grace of God for the work which they had fulfilled. And when they arrived, they gathered the church together and declared all that God had done for them, and how He had opened a door of faith to the Gentiles (Acts 14:26–27).

God prepares us for what he has prepared for us

Paul's biography reveals that God's providence had gone before him, moulding his life to give him the necessary attributes to be a Christian missionary and ambassador for Christ. Paul explained, 'But when He who had set me apart before I was born, and had called me through His grace, was pleased to reveal His Son to me, in order that I might preach Him among the Gentiles ...' (Galatians

1:15–16). Let us consider some of the various factors which Almighty God had woven into making the Apostle the person he was. Using Paul's own words, we evidence him explaining, 'I am a Jew, born at Tarsus in Cilicia, but brought up in this city [Jerusalem] at the feet of Gamaliel, educated according to the strict manner of the law of our fathers ...' (Acts 22:3). The details are important.

- As a Jew, Paul had a bridge into the Jewish world. He first made his way to the synagogues of the cities and towns he visited and would have been initially welcomed there. This gave him a platform to preach the gospel to both Jews and proselytes, and an opening to explain from the Scriptures being read that the Messiah had come in Jesus. And so, we read, for instance, that 'at Iconium they entered together into the Jewish synagogue, and so spoke that a great company believed, both of Jews and Greeks' (Acts 14:1).

- As a native of Tarsus—a mixed city of both Jews and Gentiles—Paul had also imbibed a great understanding of the culture and mind set of non-Jews, as well as his own people. Hence his suitability, under God, 'to be a minister of Christ Jesus to the Gentiles in the priestly service of the gospel of God' (Romans 15:16). When the Jews of Pisidian Antioch both rejected his message and ejected him from their synagogue, Paul said,

'Since you thrust it from you, and judge yourselves unworthy of eternal life, behold, we turn to the Gentiles' (Acts 13:46).

• Paul was steeped in the Scriptures even before his conversion—though his conversion enabled him to see the Scriptures in a new, Christ-centred light. The Scriptures, which were read in the synagogue, actually foretold that the Messiah would be the Saviour for the whole human race, not just the Hebrew race. Paul knew that he was doing the will of God by proclaiming Christ to the Gentiles. He quoted

Paul knew that he was doing the will of God by proclaiming Christ to the Gentiles.

Isaiah 49:6 to the Jews who opposed him. 'We turn to the Gentiles. For so the Lord has commanded us, saying, "I have set you to be a light to the Gentiles, that you may bring salvation to the uttermost parts of the earth"' (Acts 13:47). Hence, as Paul wrote in Romans 1:16:

> I am not ashamed of the gospel: it is the power of God for salvation to every one who has faith, to the Jew first and also to the Greek.

It is Paul's conversion and call, however, that is the key fulcrum and driving force behind his missionary endeavours. He knew the transforming power of Christ and he knew that Christ was the key to life. He could proclaim from his own and others' experiences, 'Therefore, if any one is in Christ, he is a new creation; the old has passed away, behold, the new has come' (2 Corinthians 5:17). He had been entrusted with the eternal life-giving message of the gospel. He saw himself as God's own envoy. 'So we are ambassadors for Christ, God making his appeal through us. We beseech you on behalf of Christ, be reconciled to God' (2 Corinthians 5:20). Paul would agree with Charles Wesley's hymn:

> A charge to keep I have
> A God to glorify
> A never-dying soul to save
> And fit it for the sky
> (Charles Wesley 1757–1834).

Paul the preacher

Wherever Paul went on his missionary travels, he preached. Preaching was his life's calling and work. He said, 'For Christ did not send me to baptise, but to preach the gospel' (1 Corinthians 1:17). But what was the actual contents of Paul's gospel message? Paul preached the cross of Christ and the Christ who died on the cross. His preaching was cruciform. 'We preach Christ crucified' (1 Corinthians 1:23). 'For I decided to know nothing among you except Jesus Christ and Him crucified' (1 Corinthians 2:2). Why Paul's emphasis and stress on 'the old rugged cross'?

Redemption was procured not by Christ's teaching but by His bleeding.

Because salvation was procured not by Christ's life but by His death. Redemption was procured not by Christ's teaching but by His bleeding. Paul's missionary labours, thus, had one aim: to get sinners to the foot of the cross—to urge and assist sinners to put their faith in the crucified Saviour and so be eternally saved.

'Believe in the Lord Jesus, and you will be saved' (Acts 16:31). Hence Paul was a man of a singular theme: 'Jesus Christ and Him crucified' (1 Corinthians 2:2).

Paul's only design in going to Corinth was to preach Christ; and Christ not as teacher, or as an example, or as a perfect man, or a new starting point in the development of the race—all would be mere philosophy; but Christ as crucified, that is, as dying for our sins. Christ as a propitiation was the burden of Paul's preaching. It has been well remarked that Jesus Christ refers to the person of Christ, and Him crucified to His work; which constitutes the sum of the gospel.[1]

Paul the prisoner

From the Acts of the Apostles, we see that part of Paul's missionary strategy was to visit the major cities of his day—Corinth, Philippi, Ephesus etc. These would be the places of greatest influence. In Romans 1:15 we read of him saying that 'I am eager to preach the gospel to you also who are in Rome.' No doubt he envisaged Roman soldiers, tradesmen and visitors to Rome all converted to Christ, who would then take the gospel all over the Roman Empire. Acts records that Paul's desire was granted. He did end up in Rome, but as a prisoner and not without surviving a shipwreck to get there. God moves in a mysterious way!

The last we read of Paul in Acts is his being under house arrest in Rome. But he was given liberty to preach the gospel—'testifying to the kingdom of God and trying to convince them about Jesus both from the Law of Moses and from the prophets' (Acts 28:23). From his prison in Rome, Paul wrote the epistles to the churches at Ephesus,

God moves in a mysterious way!

Colossi and Philippi. He also wrote a charming, personal letter to Philemon, encouraging him to receive back a slave of his who had absconded to Rome, and since been converted under Paul's ministry. Again, however, when the Jews—though not all—rejected Paul's message, he turned to the Gentiles saying, 'Let it be known to you then that this salvation of God has been sent to the Gentiles; they will listen' (Acts 28:28). And the book of Acts closes with Paul—in spite of his house arrest—'preaching the kingdom of God and teaching about the Lord Jesus Christ quite openly and unhindered' (Acts 28:31).

Paul the Christian martyr

We glean from Paul's second letter to Timothy that he survived his first arrest and was released to continue his endeavours for Christ. The consensus is, though, that Paul was eventually executed in Rome by the Emperor Nero in about AD 67.

In Philippians 1:23 Paul said, 'My desire is to depart and be with Christ, for that is far better.' This desire was eventually realised. Paul stayed faithful to the end. His final written words were to Timothy, Paul's young convert and assistant in the gospel. Paul knew that his death was imminent. Hence, he testified to Timothy:

> For I am already on the point of being sacrificed; the time of my departure has come. I have fought the good fight, I have finished the race, I have kept the faith. Henceforth there is laid up for me the crown of righteousness, which the Lord, the righteous judge, will award to me on that Day, and not only to me but also to all who have loved His appearing (2 Timothy 4:6–8).

I have fought the good fight, I have finished the race, I have kept the faith.

Paul was shortly beheaded. His body would have lain lifeless on the ground. Yet actually he was now more alive than ever. He was now 'away from the body and at

180

home with the Lord' (2 Corinthians 5:8) whom he had so faithfully served.

Romans:
Paul's Magnum
Opus

Paul's letter to the Romans is the clearest and most systematic explanation of the Christian gospel ever written. He wrote it from Corinth in about AD 57 during the apostle's third missionary journey. Romans elucidates the glorious Christian doctrine of justification by faith and could not be more foundational to biblical Christianity. Salvation—proclaims Paul in Romans—is by the sheer grace of God alone, achieved by Christ alone and received by faith alone. The righteousness which we lack, and the righteousness we need for the eternal wellbeing of our souls, is actually a righteousness which God in Christ graciously provides for us in the gospel, says Paul. The gospel, he says, 'is the power of God for salvation to every one who has faith ... for in it the righteousness of God is revealed through faith for faith' (Romans 1:16, 17). Justification is the grand theme of Paul's magnum opus. Christians, he explains are not guilty in the sight of God. They are right with God. They are completely righteous in the sight of God. They are justified. How is this so? Because of the complementary truths that 'they are justified by His grace' (Romans 3:24); 'justified by His blood' (Romans 5:9) and 'justified by faith' (Romans 5:1). The Christian's eternity is secure as, 'It is God who justifies; who is to condemn?' (Romans 8:33–34).

Dear Romans

Paul had not actually visited the church in Rome when he

wrote to the Roman church, but he longed and planned to do so. He confessed to them, 'I long to see you, that I may impart to you some spiritual gift to strengthen you' (Romans 1:11), and 'I am eager to preach the gospel to you also who are in Rome' (Romans 1:15). His letter to the Romans, delivered by the hand of Phoebe (Romans 16:1), paved the way for his intended visit. Phoebe could surely never have known the enormous influence that the letter she had in her hand was to have in subsequent world history. For instance, it was Martin Luther's study of Romans and his understanding of its message which led him to salvation and the assurance of salvation, and triggered off—under God—the Protestant Reformation of the 16th century. And a study of Romans today still brings us to the quintessence of the Christian gospel. Reading and re-reading it regularly repays spiritual dividends a thousand-fold.

What's it all about?

Romans consists of sixteen chapters in our English Bibles. It is Paul's lengthiest epistle. The nub of its message and theme is helpfully summarised for us in the following compact verses in Romans 3:23–25, which read:

> Since all have sinned and fall short of the glory of God, they are justified by His grace as a gift, through the redemption which is in Christ Jesus, whom God put forward as an expiation by His blood, to be received by faith.

Unpacking these very compressed verses, we note:

Justification is the grand theme of Romans. But what are we talking about when we mention Justification? A definition is helpful:

> Justification is an act of God's free grace, wherein He pardoneth all our sins and accepteth us as righteous in His sight, only for the righteousness of Christ imputed to us, and received by faith alone' (*Shorter Catechism*[1]).

Justification is the grand theme of Romans.

Lawson comments:

> Justification means pronouncing a person righteous; it is the opposite of condemnation. It is said to be an act, because it is done at once; and an act of God's free grace, because we can do nothing of ourselves to deserve it. It consists of two parts—pardon and acceptance; and we are taught the cause of it is not our own goodness, but Christ's, and that Christ's righteousness becomes ours through faith.[2]

Unpacking the nub of Paul's letter to the Romans in Romans 3:23–25, we notice:

The need for justification

'All have sinned and fall short of the glory of God' (Romans 3:23), says the Apostle. Paul actually spends the first three chapters of Romans explaining that we are all sinners, whether Jew or Gentile by birth. As sinners, we stand condemned before God. As sinners, we are not right with God. As sinners our greatest need is to be made right with God. 'None is righteous, no, not one' (Romans 3:10). We have broken God's law. We, thus, stand before Him with a guilty verdict.

As sinners our greatest need is to be made right with God.

Paul digs a deep foundation before He builds the edifice of salvation. The diagnosis precedes the cure. The law of God condemns us. We have nothing in us to plead before His bar. 'Now we know that whatever the law says it speaks to those who are under the law, so that every mouth may be stopped, and the whole world may be held accountable to God' (Romans 3:19). Is there any hope for us at all? Yes. The grace of God.

The grace of justification

'They are justified by His grace as a gift ...' (Romans 3:24). Justification is God's work, not ours, says Paul. It is by His grace, not our graft. It is a gift to be received and not a status to be achieved. It is by the sheer grace of God—His undeserved kindness, His unmerited favour, His goodness to the undeserving and even ill-deserving. Paul was supremely the apostle of divine grace. Salvation by divine grace is the distinguishing mark of biblical Christianity.

186

For by grace you have been saved through faith; and this is not your own doing, it is the gift of God— not because of works, lest any man should boast (Ephesians 2:8–9).

The testimony of every true Christian is: 'But by the grace of God I am what I am' (1 Corinthians 15:10) and will always be so. 'Where sin increased, grace abounded all the more' (Romans 5:20).

Naught have I gotten but what I received
Grace has bestowed it since I have believed
Boasting excluded, pride I abase
I'm only a sinner, saved by grace

Only a sinner, saved by grace!
Only a sinner, saved by grace
This is my story—to God be the glory—
I'm only a sinner, saved by grace.
(James Martin Gray 1851–1935).

The grounds of justification

The Christian's justification, Paul says, is based solely on what Christ has done. It is 'through the redemption which is in Christ Jesus' (Romans 3:24). To redeem means 'to pay the price' or 'to buy back' or 'to set free'. At Calvary, Christ paid the price for the believer's sins. At Calvary He paid the penalty which we owe for breaking God's law. Christ died at Calvary to free us from the condemnation we deserve for our sins. And He did this by taking the condemnation we deserve upon Himself, in our room and stead. Paul goes on to explain, '... Christ Jesus, whom God put forward as a propitiation by His blood' (Romans 3:24–25, ESV). It was the love of God which provided Christ to meet our deepest need to be right with Himself. 'God shows His love for us in that while we were yet sinners Christ died for us' (Romans 5:8). We have already considered that propitiation refers to the turning aside of divine wrath. At Calvary, Christ satisfied God's justice. He endured the wrath of God which is our due to save us from the wrath of God which is our due. Calvary is therefore the

> ***At Calvary, Christ satisfied God's justice.***

supreme demonstration of both the love of God and the righteousness of God—His wrath in punishing sin, and His mercy in pardoning the sinner—'that He Himself is righteous and that He justifies him who has faith in Jesus' (Romans 3:26).

The means of justification

How does the blessing of justification become our own? How is the blessing of justification received? How do we become right with God in our personal experience? By faith in the Lord Jesus Christ, says Paul—'whom God put forward as a propitiation by His blood, to be received by faith' (Romans 3:25 ESV).

At the outset of this chapter, we saw that 'Justification

by Faith' is the grand, overarching theme of Romans. What then is faith? Faith is simply the human channel or instrument by which we receive the blessing of God. It is the spoon by which we eat the food! We are saved by God's grace in Christ, not faith. Yet paradoxically there is also no salvation apart from saving faith in the crucified Christ:

> A man is not justified by works of the law but through faith in Jesus Christ, even we have believed in Christ Jesus in order to be justified by faith in Christ, and not by works of the law, because by works of the law shall no one be justified (Galatians 2:16).

> For we hold that a man is justified by faith apart from works of law (Romans 3:28).

> To one who does not work but trusts Him who justifies the ungodly, his faith is reckoned as righteousness (Romans 4:5).

> Q. What is faith in Jesus Christ?
> A. Faith in Jesus Christ is a saving grace, whereby we receive and rest upon Him alone for salvation, as He is offered to us in the gospel (*Shorter Catechism*[3]).

Salvation by grace and salvation by faith are thus complementary, not contradictory truths. Christ alone saves, yet there is no salvation apart from a personal, faith union with Christ—apprehending Him. It is faith which unites us to Him. It is by faith that we receive all His saving blessings and benefits. In the New Testament, faith in Christ, trusting Christ, receiving Christ and believing in Christ are synonymous. Christians are known as 'the faithful'. Christians are also known as 'believers'.

> Faith is a living power from heaven
> Which grasps the promise God has given
> Securely fixed on Christ alone
> A trust that cannot be o'er thrown
>
> Faith finds in Christ whate'er we need
> To save and strengthen, guide and feed
> Strong in His grace, it joys to share
> His cross, in hope His crown to wear
> (P Herbert, 1533–71).

Justification

Justification. It is a legal term. It takes us into the law courts. It refers to God's own verdict—His acceptance of the sinner as righteous, not on the grounds of their own righteousness but Christ's. Christ lived a sinless life. Christ died an atoning death so that the believer might be justified. God credits—imputes—the righteousness of Christ to all who believe in Him.

> For our sake He made Him to be sin who knew no sin, so that in Him we might become the righteousness of God (2 Corinthians 5:21).

Justification is the theme of Paul's magnum opus—

his letter to the Romans. Romans is the nearest we will ever get to a Christian manifesto. Paul describes this as 'my gospel' (Romans 2:16). It is the 'gospel of Christ' (2 Corinthians 9:13) and 'the gospel of God' (Romans 1:1)—'the glorious gospel of the blessed God with which I have been entrusted' (1 Timothy 1:11). It is the only way of salvation. It is the only solid ground for the soul's eternal wellbeing, as, to be justified by God's grace in Christ is to be eternally saved, eternally safe and eternally secure.

To be justified by God's grace in Christ is to be eternally saved, eternally safe and eternally secure.

The Book of
Revelation
AD 95

Chapter 20

All will be well

The last book of the Bible—the book of Revelation—assures us that, whatever our current circumstances, and whatever is going on in the world around us, all will be eternally well. Revelation assures and reassures us of the ultimate triumph of God's purposes of grace and glory. He cannot be thwarted or defeated. His will, will be done. Paradise lost will most certainly be Paradise restored in God's due time. The Lord Jesus Christ shall triumph. He shall come again in glory and make all things new, and His people—His bride—will share in His ultimate and eternal victory in a renewed universe, and enjoy His fellowship for ever more.

John: not as young as he was

The book of Revelation is what it says: a revelation. It is an unveiling of the triumph of the Lord Jesus Christ and His lordship of history. It begins: 'The revelation of Jesus Christ, which God gave Him to show to His servants what must soon take place' (Revelation 1:1). The book was written by the Apostle John in about AD 95, when the Christian church was undergoing severe persecution. The aged John, himself, was separated from Christian fellowship, and exiled on the Isle of Patmos for his faith. Yet, while there, he received the most remarkable vision. The risen, reigning, glorified Lord Jesus Christ, whom He had known on earth, appeared to him in an astonishing way. John's discouragement within and chaos without notwithstanding, Jesus' voice sounded out. He had everything covered.

Fear not, I am the first and the last and the living one; I died and behold I am alive for evermore, and I have the keys of Death and Hades (Revelation 1:17–18).

The book of Revelation fits into the category known as apocalyptic literature. John's vision is given in picture language, making much use of symbols and imagery. It is easy to get lost in the details, but if we keep three main images, which John employs, in mind, it will be easier to steer a course through the book of Revelation. These three images are The Throne, The Lamb and The Dragon.

The throne

In his remarkable vision, John relates that, 'At once I was in the Spirit, and lo, a throne stood in heaven, with one seated on the throne!' (Revelation 4:2). The throne is a symbol of kingship, rule and authority. The ultimate king and authority is Almighty God Himself. John's vision of the throne was to assure his readers both then and now that, the rampant evil around us notwithstanding, God is in control. He is on the throne and can never be overthrown. The absolute sovereignty of God—the God-ness of God—

God is in control. He is on the throne and can never be overthrown.

truth be told, is the only true and ultimate comfort for the troubled soul. God has all things covered. Nothing takes Him by surprise. Not even the devil himself can 'get one over' Him. The sovereignty of God is a main theme of Revelation, as it is of the whole Bible. 'Hallelujah! For the Lord our God the Almighty reigns' (Revelation 19:6):

> The Lord is King! Lift up your voice
> O earth and all ye heavens, rejoice!
> From world to world the joy shall ring
> The Lord omnipotent is King!
>
> He reigns! Ye saints exalt your strains
> Your God is King, your Father reigns
> And He is at the Father's side
> The Man of love, the Crucified
> (Josiah Conder 1789–1855).

The Lamb

Central to the last book of the Bible, as to the whole Bible is 'the Lamb'. John wrote how, 'I saw a Lamb standing, as though it had been slain' (Revelation 5:6). He notices also that worship is offered to this Lamb, who is shown to be co-equal with God the Father. 'To Him who sits upon the throne and to the Lamb be blessing and honour and glory and might for ever and ever!' (Revelation 5:13). The Lamb refers to none other than the Lord Jesus Christ. The title is a loaded one. It was a lamb which brought redemption from Egypt in Old Testament times, and it is the death of the Lord Jesus—the Lamb—in New Testament times which has wrought the eternal redemption of God's people. In his Gospel, John noted that, when Jesus was on earth, John the Baptist pointed to Him and proclaimed, 'Behold, the Lamb of God who takes away the sin of the world!' (John 1:29). The last book of the Bible depicts the final and ultimate triumph of the Lamb. John's describing of His breaking of the seals of the scroll of time reveals He is the Lord of history. His death

The last book of the Bible depicts the final and ultimate triumph of the Lamb.

and resurrection guarantees the security of all who belong to Him. John writes, 'Then I looked, and ... on Mount Zion stood the Lamb, and with Him a hundred and forty-four thousand who had His name and His Father's name written on their foreheads' (Revelation 14:1). There were twelve tribes of Israel—God's Old Testament people—and there were twelve disciples of Christ, God's embryonic New Testament people. Twelve times twelve is a hundred and forty-four. Here, then, the hundred and forty-four thousand refers to the sum total of all those redeemed by Christ. They are saved and safe. They owe their all to Christ. Hence, they 'follow the Lamb wherever He goes; these have been redeemed from mankind as first fruits for God and the Lamb' (Revelation 14:4).

The dragon

Revelation in many respects takes us behind the scenes. It reveals that the evil in the world is due to the activity of Satan, the enemy of God and His people. Revelation depicts him as a fierce and fearsome dragon. Yet, while he is mighty, he is not all-mighty. His power and activity are limited by God. Yet his presence is included in Scripture as a warning to God's people. It behoves us not to be 'ignorant of his designs' (2 Corinthians 2:11). John describes him as, 'a great red dragon, with seven heads and ten horns, and seven diadems upon his heads' (Revelation 12:3). Who is this dragon? He is 'the great dragon ... who is called the Devil and Satan, the deceiver of the whole world' (Revelation 12:9). He is shown in Revelation 12 as attempting to destroy the people of God, making 'war ... on those who keep the commandments of God and bear testimony to Jesus' (Revelation 12:17). But his power to carry out his intentions was and is limited and thwarted.

Satan—in the book of Revelation—is shown to use many guises. In chapter 13 he appears as 'a beast rising out of the sea' (Revelation 13:1). This refers to the anti-God governments that persecute the people of God, in John's day and now. In Revelation 13:11 he is also shown as 'another beast which rose out of the earth'—referring to the false religions around in John's day and ours, all of which seek to allure the people of God, either by brute force or subtle seduction. In Revelation 17, Satan is shown as using the guise of, if you will, a great harlot—'a woman sitting on a scarlet beast' (Revelation 17:3). This woman has great power—the power of both seduction, persecution and harm. A prostitute seeks to promote immorality and unfaithfulness. But God's people are called to be faithful to Him through thick and thin and resist the devil in all his guises. Revelation 17, though, tells us that all these evil forces 'are of one mind ... they will make war on the Lamb, and the Lamb will conquer them for He is Lord of lords and King of kings ...' (Revelation 17:13, 14).

But God's people are called to be faithful to Him through thick and thin and resist the devil in all his guises.

Revelation, then, is a call to realism. Satan is a force to be reckoned with, but we must not lose heart. God's purposes will prevail. The city of Babylon—a worldly city contrary to all that is of God—will be destroyed, and eventually, 'the devil ...' will be 'thrown into the lake of fire and sulphur ... and ... be tormented day and night for ever and ever' (Revelation 20:10).

In Eden, it was the devil who tempted Eve and so triggered the Fall with all its consequences. Revelation reveals that one day God will fully and finally overthrow the devil, and Paradise will be restored.

Paradise restored

The Bible begins—as we have seen—in the Garden of Eden. This was the most perfect environment, and our first ancestors enjoyed unblemished fellowship with God. But this was all forfeited by sin. Fellowship with God was spoiled, and expulsion from the Garden occurred. The Bible, however, also ends in a garden. Revelation tells us of the Garden City of the New Jerusalem. Paradise will be restored! In this Garden City we glimpse again 'the tree of life with its twelve kinds of fruit, yielding its fruit each month; and the leaves of the tree were for the healing of the nations' (Revelation 22:2). Here is Edenic restoration! Here is creation perfected. Here is full salvation.

The last book of the Bible reveals that the redemption, which Christ procured for His people at Calvary, will one day culminate in their living in 'a new heaven and a new earth; for the first heaven and the first earth had passed away' (Revelation 21:1). The universe will be recreated, and God's people will dwell there with Him in new, glorious, immortal bodies, in which they will 'serve Him day and night within His temple ... They shall hunger no more, neither thirst any more' (Revelation 7:15, 16). They will be eternally saved, safe, secure and satisfied, and finally able to fulfil their chief end of glorifying God and enjoying Him for ever, free from all that hinders and handicaps us from doing so in this current, fallen age.

What will life be like in the 'new heaven and [the] new earth'? It will be greater than words can describe or for our current capacity to comprehend. John describes it as a joyful wedding feast, with God's people 'prepared as a bride adorned for her husband' (Revelation 21:2). 'Let us rejoice and exult and give Him the glory, for the marriage of the Lamb has come …' (Revelation 19:7).

What won't be there

John also describes the consummation of the Christian's salvation by telling us what will not be part of the future glory as well as what will be. In the age to come, certain things will be—thankfully—gone for ever:

- There will be no more tears, for God 'will wipe away every tear from their eyes' (Revelation 21:4).
- There will be no more death—death being God's judgement on sin—for 'death shall be no more' nor consequently shall there be 'mourning nor crying' (Revelation 21:4).
- There shall not be 'pain any more, for the former things have passed away' (Revelation 21:4). This includes all physical, mental, psychological and spiritual pain.
- 'There shall be no night there' (Revelation 21:25). There was much fear of darkness in Bible times, before the days of electricity and the neon bulb. Darkness signified evil and terror. Hence, in the

age to come all darkness will be banished. It is incompatible with God's eternal kingdom of light. 'The city has no need of sun or moon to shine upon it, for the glory of God is its light and its lamp is the Lamb' (Revelation 21:23).

- John also noticed that 'the sea was no more' (Revelation 21:1). It was the sea which separated John from his friends, exiled as he was on the Isle of Patmos. The age to come, therefore, is an age of reconciliation. The sea in the biblical mind-set also did not have our western, pleasurable connotations. The sea to them spelled danger and uncontrolled, wild restlessness. 'The wicked are like the tossing sea; for it cannot rest, and its waters toss up mire and dirt' (Isaiah 57:20). In glory, the chaos of this age will give way to calm.

Those who believe in Jesus are freed from the curse, and will be so for ever.

And in the age to come 'there shall no more be anything accursed' (Revelation 22:3). The curse refers to the judgment of God. The gospel proclaims, however, that, 'Christ redeemed us from the curse of the law, having become a curse for us ...' (Galatians 3:13). Those who believe in Jesus are freed from the curse, and will be so for ever ...

O sweet and blessed country
The home of God's elect

> O sweet and blessed country
> That eager hearts expect
> Jesus, in mercy bring us
> To that dear land of rest
> Who art with God the Father
> And Spirit, ever blest!
> (Bernard of Cluny, dates unknown)

The best of all is God is with us

Finally, John reveals that the true blessedness of the age to come is this: God Himself. His covenant of grace will then be fulfilled. He will be our God and we shall be His people. 'He will dwell with them, and they shall be His people and God Himself will be with them' (Revelation 21:3). True blessedness is knowing God. True blessedness is fellowship with God. True blessedness is eternal life— enjoying God, serving God and rejoicing in His presence.

> *True blessedness is eternal life— enjoying God, serving God and rejoicing in His presence.*

> This is eternal life, that they know Thee the only true God and Jesus Christ whom Thou hast sent (John 17:3).

> In Thy presence there is fullness of joy, in Thy right hand are pleasures for evermore (Psalm 16:11).

Paradise Lost will therefore yet be Paradise Restored.

For the Christian, the best is yet to be. The sufferings of this present time are not worth comparing with the glory that is to be revealed to us (Romans 8:18).

> What no eye has seen, nor ear heard, nor the heart of man conceived, what God has prepared for those who love Him (1 Corinthians 2:9).

And when will all this occur? It will occur when the Lord Jesus Christ comes again in power and great glory. He still reminds us 'Behold, I make all things new' (Revelation 21:5). His last words in the Bible—and the penultimate verse of the whole Bible, are these:

> Surely I am coming soon (Revelation 22:20).

Hence the longing and prayer of Christians today and throughout the ages has been the same.

Amen. Come, Lord Jesus! (Revelation 22:20).

To Him be the glory forever!

Soli Deo Gloria

Endnotes

Ch. 1 Adam and Eve

1   Roderick Lawson, *The Shorter Catechism with Scripture Proofs and Comments*, (Edinburgh: Knox Press, 1988), Q.1, p.7

Ch. 2 Noah and the Great Flood

1   Roderick Lawson, *The Shorter Catechism with Scripture Proofs and Comments*, Q.14, p.14

2   *The Lion Concise Bible Encyclopaedia*, (Tring: Lion Publishing, 1980) p.313

Ch. 3 The Patriarchs

1   Roderick Lawson, *The Shorter Catechism with Scripture Proofs and Comments*, Q.11, p.12

Ch. 14 The Birth of the Lord Jesus Christ

1   Ibid., Q.21, 22, p.18

2   James Montgomery (1821), 'Hail to the Lord's Anointed', https://hymnary.org/text/hail_to_the_lords_anointed. Sourced: 7/12/21

3   Roderick Lawson, *The Shorter Catechism with Scripture Proofs and Comments*, Q.26, p.21

4   Ibid., Q.26, p.21

Ch. 15 The Death of Christ

1   Ibid., Q.25, p.20

Ch. 16 The Resurrection of Christ

1   Ibid., Q.38, p.29

Ch. 17 The Coming of the Holy Spirit

1   Ibid., Q. 29, p. 23
2   Ibid., Q. 31, p. 24
3   Ibid., Q. 89, p. 52

Ch. 18 Paul

1   Hodge, cited in: Geoffrey B. Wilson, *1 Corinthians*, (Edinburgh: Banner of Truth, 1978), p. 38

Ch. 19 Romans—Paul's Magnum Opus

1   Roderick Lawson, *The Shorter Catechism with Scripture Proofs and Comments*, Q. 33, p. 25
2   Ibid., Q. 33, p. 25
3   Ibid., Q 86, p. 50